Embodying

Meditati

Realization ن Tranquility

In Daily Living

By Christopher J. Smith

Embodying The Secret Self

Christopher J. Smith
Paperback edition first published in Great Britain in 2018
eBook edition first published in Great Britain in 2018

ISBN: 9781788083959

Acknowledgements and Dedication

My sincere gratitude goes out to all of the enlightened beings throughout the ages, and recent past who have contributed to the teachings, methods and pointers that I now share with you in the pages of this book. May the source that is in them be recognised and awoken within you eternally.

I thank all of you who have the courage to question what you have been taught, and whom seek reality and the eternal essence of who you really are. With persistence and surrender...freedom will be realized.

Life is just a play.

Enjoy the ride!

I am another you.
With gratitude.
Christopher

Introduction – Embodying The Teachings of The Secret Self

Section 1 – Self-Realization And The Timeless Dimension

Section 2 - Awakening Through Conscious Practice & Meditation

Section 3 - Relationships And Communication For Self-Realization

Section 4 - The Joy Of Being In Action

Section 5 - Devotion & Surrender To The Infinite - The Final Enlightened Liberation

Introduction

Before the creation of the book *'The Secret Self - A Practical Guide To Spiritual Awakening And Inner Freedom'* I had a strong vision to design a practical pocketbook that people could carry with them everywhere in order to practice the teachings of meditation and Self-Realization in everyday life. It was my knowing that if Self-Realization is to truly become a direct moment to moment embodied experience, that it must not only be practiced in the corner of a quiet room somewhere, but that it must also penetrate every area of our day to day living experience. Otherwise, meditation and daily living can end up becoming separated and then so can your life and the expression of your true nature; with spirituality becoming something you only embody when you're alone and not at work or in the presence of others.

And so, while sitting meditation practice is extremely powerful *(and recommended in the book – The Secret Self)*, what is equally or even more powerful, is bringing your practice into everyday situations - and this is really where the rubber meets the road! This is truly what Enlightenment and Self-Realization is all about. It's about us waking up to reality in the present and becoming that free bright light of change and transformation in the world that we all are. If your freedom and tranquility does not include being free and tranquil everywhere at each moment, then it is not true freedom and tranquility at all. It is only conditional and limited.

The original idea of the first book was to be a practical pocketbook guide; however when I began writing it soon turned into a book just under 400 pages! And so now with people asking for a shorter version of the original, I feel it is time to release a practical pocketbook manual of the core teachings and meditations within the original Secret Self Book, and so this book *'Embodying The Secret Self - Meditations for Self-Realization & Tranquility in Daily Living'* is just that. This book is where the hammer meets the nail, where we can practice and recognize our true nature and reality in our moment to moment living experience. This book can also act as an introduction to the bigger book *'The Secret Self'*.

This book is not a means of *'becoming'* but a means of *'recognition'*. It is a practical way of turning our awareness towards the reality of what is already presently here: that being our true **Infinite nature** and reality *'as it is'* in its purest form. Human consciousness and civilization is at a current crossroads in history. Many beings are raising their consciousness, while at the same time the world is facing extreme challenge after extreme challenge. It is now, during these times on earth, that this book is needed more than ever. It is for each and every being on the planet, because when it comes down to it, all of our issues all come from the same root – **mental programming**.

At this time, being in contact with reality is needed more than ever. We can either awaken fully from the dream of unconscious programming, or fall further and further asleep into it; this is a choice we each have, a choice which can only be made **NOW**.

The actual experience of awakening can only happen in the present.

Within this book are the practices, methods and pointers that can lead one to an experience of the **Secret Self** beyond the level of mind: a direct awakening beyond thought. There are short passage's that can be read as *pointers* towards inner silence and a form of meditative reading that brings one to the experience of **Self-Transcendence**. Feel free to take your time and **pause** at each passage to allow **inner spaciousness** to arise. Use each meditation as a moment to moment practice as you go about the day.

It is recommended to stick with one practice for a significant amount of time, and then intuitively move onto the next when it feels right. Each practice, if done with full consciousness will bring you to the experience of being **aware here-now** and will bring the direct experience of the **Secret Self** (*Your True Nature*). In this way each practice alone has the **power** and **potency** to bring one to Enlightenment (*Self-Realization*), which really means to be fully awake in the here and now. This brings one a great immeasurable freedom. Freedom which can lead to peace, tranquility, joy, bliss and even ecstasy.

Enjoy the mystery that unfolds, because you are the **Infinite... all that is**, and all that is needed is to directly experience it consciously to awaken.

Section 1
Self-Realization And
The Timeless Dimension

1 - Your Original Enlightened Nature

*You are the **Infinite-Self**. All is the Infinite-Self and the Infinite-Self is all.*

In the beginning of existence your nonphysical nature as the **'one Infinite Self '**, as the **origin** of all things, as pure possibility and potentiality, gave rise to the seemingly physical solid manifest world. What sprang forth were a multiplicity of unique expressions all emanating from and containing the same source running through them. This core essence or substratum level that is both **in** and **as** all things is the **immanence** of existence: life's fundamental and immediate nature. It is a **space** that simultaneously interpenetrates and holds everything together and within it.

You are like that space in which everything occurs.

You are like that space in which all experiences visit and depart.

You are like that space in which space itself is seen.

You are like that space in which even space itself rests.

The space which is seen is like the same space which is looking.

See if you can find the line which separates the two.

See if you can find the space within by first noticing the empty space in-between all objects.

*To go even deeper to the Infinite-Self, see what it is that is **watchful** of both inner and outer spaciousness, find that which notices both.*

After the multiplicities were formed, the Infinite-Self began to experience being a **finite**-self by becoming lost in a dream. A dream of **identity** as the very form it gave birth to: a dream made of thought. This thought-made dream is what is referred to as **unconsciousness**, because when one is lost in **thinking** they are in a hazy **hypnotic** state of unawareness. Not fully conscious or aware of the true reality of existence in the present, instead only living in the collected information of the past. In its formation, the Infinite-Self became so fixated and amazed with the temporary appearances of the world, material, sensory, pleasure and other-wise, that it forgot itself and fell into the conditioned-mind with a deep fascination. From here, a finite-identity was born in which all things were then seen through the lens of **thought** *(the past)*, thus creating limitation.

When thinking is identified with who you are, then you become immersed in the mind. From here, all thoughts that arise become recognized as yourself. If one *thought* is identified with, then it would continuously be **thought time and time again**. If it is seen to be a true depiction of reality *(a true thought)* it becomes a belief, with the belief then becoming a strong personal inner experience and conviction. When you believe something, it becomes your internal experience and the lens through which you see the world. In the same way that one can dream at night and can believe the dream to be real, so too does the Infinite-Self. That is, through the medium of the conditioned-mind, it thinks and experiences itself to be finite. **Awakening** means to wake up from this illusory **day-dream** created by the mind and meet face to face with the source of infinity that is in and all around you. **Self-realization is not a becoming, it is not a step towards something greater, it is the immediate and direct recognition of your inherent greatness as the Infinite source of all existence right now.** Your true self is boundless and completely free. It is beyond limits and identity. Despite the finite dream of a smaller personal self, the Infinite bigger Self is always there watching the dream occurring inside of it.

The small me is happening inside the greater me, just as a night time dream happens in the head...

What you essentially are – *a being of Infinite Greatness* - is always there waiting for you to turn and recognize it, in the present. It wants you to connect with reality and become aware of your natural enlightened state.

However in order to connect, we must move beyond the conditioned state the mind and thinking. Don't try to understand the Infinite-Self with the mind, that is impossible, as how can something that is finite possibly understand the Infinite?! It is like an ant trying to understand the whole cosmos.

Don't try to think about it or grasp it with the mind, the mind is not the tool for the job. Instead, simply turn to recognize it directly within your present experience by means of inner **watchfulness**. That is the only way to see reality **as it is**, and to see the true self as you are, is to drop thought and look through means of a clear **thoughtless awareness**.

This is the difference between the intellect and direct experience. The former is only ever a concept about something, whereas direct experience is the embodiment of it, it is immediate contact with reality. This book is all about you having a direct experience of reality, as this is the only way to truly awaken.

Recognize the truth of who you are **now** in this moment and see that you are that which is free beyond the mind and beyond the dream. See the one who is the **witness** of all experiences and transient phenomena.

When self-identity in thought ceases, Enlightenment just is.

Just be aware here now.

Just be.

2 - The Awakening Beyond Thought

Awakening beyond thought is the first step to lasting freedom.

Enlightened beings throughout the ages have always asked one pertinent question that led them to Self-Realization: *'**Who am I truly**?'*

It's an age old question that most beings never ask or ever find the answer to, and so even for the few people that do ask it, most eventually give up. The few that continue to ask the question however, eventually find the answer - but never in the way that they might expect. The answer is never intellectual: rather it is a **pointer** taking you beyond the intellect and towards the **direct experience** of one's true enlightened nature. The question is not a problem to solve but is instead a sign post, where it points but never claims to be what it is.

As we practice **embodying the Secret Self**, we should have this question somewhere in the background as a means of reference and remembrance of what we truly are. We cannot come to know this by way of *'thought'* but instead only by way of **stillness** *(inner quietness)*, **insight** *(inner-sight)* and **hereness** *(being present to the moment)*. The question keeps us on track for when we stray back into fascination with the mind. I say **when**, because it will inevitably happen many times over. The whole awakening process is a game of continually moving back into full **present consciousness** whenever we become **unconscious** (*lost in the inner mental conversations*), until eventually we fall into unconsciousness no more and make our whole life a fully conscious existence (*always consciously present and aware*).

Whenever we appear to lose ourselves and slip back into unconsciousness, we can ask this question to direct us back home. What is our home?

Our home is when we are **consciously aware** in the **present**. This question of '*Who am I truly?*' is what will act as a **pointer** and **reminder** for us to navigate back to our true nature in times of unconscious **hypnotic thinking.**

To ask this question on its own, can bring us to the immediate experience of being consciously aware in the **here** and **now**.

If you ever feel lost in your daily practice and find yourself falling back into unconsciousness, rest assured that you can always return by asking yourself this key question.

It is handy to keep this question (*quest*) in your back pocket as a marker or reference for the '*path*' that you are on. The path being – to awaken from thought into the Infinite-Self (*Secret Self*), which is the meaning of **Spiritual Awakening** and **Enlightenment**. It's the path from illusion to reality, or in other words, from the programmed-mind into the clarity of present moment awareness.

The beginning of Self-Realization and freedom is to notice... that who you are is that which is **aware** of thinking and not thinking itself. It is to notice a thought and then notice that it is **noticing** the thought. Self-Realization means to wake up beyond thought and being the **thinker** of thoughts.

Prior to thought there is a substratum dimension of **quiet intelligence** from which all thought appears from and subsides back into.

All thoughts emerge from silence and then fall back into silence. Who you are is the **witness** to both silence and no-mind as well as thought and the active mind.

Practical Exercise: *Take a moment of inner quiet and see if you can* **observe** *a thoughts appearance and disappearance in the mind right now...*
When a thought appears, there is a **witness** present within you that is able to watch it. When the thought disappears the witness of it still remains...

Awakening beyond the dream of thought is a giant leap into the pure reality of boundless spacious intelligence. When you become a witness to thought, in that act **Self-Transcendence** will happen instant-aneously. Self-Transcendence occurs when we realize that the finite-self is made up of nothing but thoughts. When we observe these thoughts, we automatically break free from the realm of the limited and position ourselves in the throne of the Infinite Unlimited Self.

It is our conviction of being a finite-self and the belief in thoughts which creates the day-dream of being a separate entity from the rest of existence. We wake up from this dream by finding that we are the one that the dream is happening in front of and inside of, not the one it is happening to. *There is a witnessing that all thinking reports to. Can you look within now and witness this witnessing?*

The world of mind, just like the world of form is always forever changing, while our true selves remain changeless. When you become aware and identify the constant within you, you will find everlasting life. So what is it in us, which never changes?

Awareness, awareness, awareness is the prime ele-ment that never ceases. The witness - just like **awareness** - is the quality of being aware. They are two words pointing to the same essence. Awareness is not a thought, it is a **silent sensing** of one's present exper-ience. We can experience the reality of our unchanging awareness both directly and by reflection. Think back to when you were a child. **Who** was it in **you** that was having that experience then? Were you aware? Please look...

Now try to recall the time when you were a teenager. Who was it in you that were having that experience then? Were you also aware then? Please observe...

And so, who is it that is having this experience right now? Are you aware right now? Please see...

You see, there has always been an element constantly within you that has remained static, while all other things on the surface have changed. Your thoughts and beliefs have changed over time, and your body has changed over time, yet the *'direct experiencer'* within you, has always been there through all your life's ups, downs and changes.

Can you be aware of this **'direct experiencer'** that has always been present? Please look now...

Practical Exercise: *See if you can be aware of this ever-present element within you in which all phenomena and experiences are appearing in front of and report to. Do this now.*

Identify the changeless within you and you will find the immortal at the base of all life. When you rise above thought a whole new experience of life becomes available. True reality becomes your nature, and inner freedom your direct experience. Every phenomenon in the so called *'physical world'* is **impermanent**. That is, it is always moving and changing and it never stays the same. It is born and then it dies. Yet within you, there is that which has never been born or ever dies: your **immortal unborn nature** which exists beyond the realm of time and space.

It has always been there, it will forever be there, and it is there right now. Look now and see...

3 - Asleepness And Ignorance: Causes Of Suffering And Self-Imposed Limitations

All suffering begins from ignorance of the truth.

The opposite of asleepness is wakefulness. Wakefulness means to be conscious without being **lost** in thinking.

When we are consumed by thinking we fall back into the **unconscious** state of the mind, and this is what is referred to as **asleepness**.

The cure is to become consciously aware in this moment, and to continually do so. Being present and aware to the here and now is wakefulness - and this is what it means to be awakened. Awakening is awareness of the here and now. Awakening is awareness of thought and non-indulgence in thought.

Awakening means to ultimately be aware of every-thing in your immediate experience, without an ounce of unconsciousness.

This unawareness of our true nature is what is meant by the term *'ignorance'*. Ignorance simply means **'not to know'**; that is, not to know who we are beyond unconsciousness and thought. When we don't know who we truly are we suffer and tend to cause suffering for others - often unconsciously. By not knowing our true nature we play out unconscious conditioned behaviors, and identify them as our own.

For example, society may have told us, or led us to believe we are, or *'should be'* a certain way, when in fact, we are not. The people in our lives may have influenced us to value or believe particular things, simply through exposure to their thoughts or be-havior. We may believe something about ourselves based on past experiences *(which can taint the lens of the present)* which also aren't true. This conditioning happens for most people all of the time, and many live in a state of unconsciousness and ignorance for most of their lives. And so, a world of people not knowing their Infinite nature is a world of suffering and self-imposed limitation.

Suffering and self-imposed limitation ends when the dream of being isolated is exposed. When we are no longer ignorant of our ultimate nature, a whole new dimension of life becomes known in our immediate experience. All ugliness of conditioning and separation moves far away and we are met by the love, joy and beauty of our pure natural existence in the present.

There is and has been so much suffering in the world, and this suffering that we see first began as suffering and ignorance within humanity's individual and collective unconsciousness. All of the mayhem, mischief, conflict and suffering are a direct result of the ignorance of our true nature and our own inner suffering projected onto the world.

When we do not know the true nature of ourselves and others, this results in us doing horrendous things to each other and ourselves through this ignorance. We only have to look at history to see this. This unawareness of our real self also limits and binds us to certain ways of perceiving and experiencing. It is the discovery of our ultimate nature that holds the key to ending this suffering and limitation. Suffering will only truly end when ignorance of who we are ends.

Our inner awakening is the beginning of truth and freedom and therefore the end of suffering and ignorance.

The light that is revealed through inner awakening will chase away the darkness of ignorance and put an end to any inner turmoil we may have. As we awaken to deeper levels of truth, joy and true lasting happiness begins to flower within our hearts and radiates outwards to those around us.

Through the realization of ultimate reality, our whole experience of life becomes enhanced, and a whole new world emerges for us.

A thought believed and identified with as who we are creates a feeling, and this feeling flavors our experience of self and the world. If we think and feel negative and alone, then all of a sudden, the world seems a lonely and unpleasant place. If we think and feel angry, then everyone we see seems angry or upset and the whole world can seem drenched in it. A thought believed is dangerous. It is a distortion of our true undiluted reality.

Practical Exercise: *Begin to take thoughts less seriously, don't believe every thought that passes through the mind.*

One of the biggest discoveries you may come to see is that no thought is, or ever can be true. A thought is always a limited description of something that is unlimited. It is always a concept about something that is not conceptual. It always creates a meaning where there is no inherent meaning.

All thought is just a superimposed mind-based reality placed on top of the actual reality itself. It is simply thoughts made of language: a language that is not original to who we really are, rather a language that we were given and taught. In essence, all language is a communication tool which has been invented, agreed to, and of which we ascribe meaning to. Ultimately, it cannot give true meaning to life, as meaning only comes in the absence of thought.

In other words, reality is true and pure until it is dist-orted by the filter of mind and thought. No thought is true because no thought can truly encapsulate the vastness of reality.

So with our thoughts and words just being agree-ments of a society for communication purposes, they are therefore useless when it comes to understanding reality. The **Isness** of life cannot be described. To try and describe it is to limit it - and the moment you limit it, you lose its true unlimited nature.

If you deeply understand this truth, then it will change everything. No longer will your thoughts be taken as gospel truth: instead you will take them less seriously and be free. Instead of seeking to understand reality through the lens of thinking, you will put thinking to one side and make contact with reality, directly.

Truth is experiential not intellectual.

In this way you will come to see suffering is only ever optional, as it is a mind created phenomena. Pain will happen for sure, but suffering is a matter of what we believe and tell ourselves about the pain. Suffering is an inner commentary of experiences. It is a mental thought-based script of resistance **about how things are** in this moment. It is the habit of our conditioned thinking which tries to create a meaning where there isn't one. There is something much more profound than a mind-made meaning, and that is the Isness of reality itself, which is always neutral and pure.

The same holds true for **self-imposed limitations**. A self-imposed limitation comes in the form of a mental story and belief. It may say things like - *'I can't do this'* or *'I'm not good enough'*, as just two common examples. It will always come as a doubt, or as fear disguised as practicality. Without the belief in the mental script, where would a self-imposed limitation be?

It is only the belief in thought that may hold one back from their unlimited potential and ultimate freedom.

What would you be without the thought or belief?

What would you be without the mental commentary?

Contemplate these things.

4 - The Mind is a Collection

All thoughts are the same thoughts recycled by the collective mind.

One of the greatest realizations that exists for us, is when we discover that the mind is not our own. Rather, that the mind is a collection and agreement that belongs to the collective mind.

All thought is made of language. If you are German you will have thoughts in German, if you are French you will think in French, if English you think in English, and so forth. Without language you cannot think, because thought is comprised primarily of language. Language which we now know is an agreement and not inherent in the actual fabric of reality.

The other component of thought is imagination. Even imagination is only a collection of outside things that you have seen previously, as you cannot imagine what you have never seen. Whatever you imagine will always be made of bits and pieces of information you have observed at some point in your life, which you subsequently remember and recall through memory. So all thought is nothing more than a collection of past information gathered from the outside world. What this means is that all mind has been given to you externally and no thought is original to who you essentially are.

You are the watcher of thoughts not the thoughts themselves.

All mind and thought is the past. It belongs to the world of the changing forms. To the world of the mortal, and you are not mortal but the **immortal**. There is no such thing as an original thought. Any thought that has ever passed through your head has passed through thousands or millions of heads beforehand. All the thoughts in the world are recycled thoughts.

When you start to see that the mind is not who you really are, you begin to take the mind less seriously. The result of this is less suffering and more joy, peace and freedom - and a great inner spaciousness occurs naturally. A true intelligence emerges. In the absence of thought we find true love, and this love is the total inclusiveness of life.

When your identity with the mind ends, you stop looking to the mind for answers and instead start living more spontaneously and naturally from a place of inner silence. You begin to see reality *'as it is'* as opposed to the thoughts about it. You make true contact with reality through **firsthand** experience as opposed to a secondhand experience that is derived from the mind.

The information of the mind can only ever be secondhand. It is someone else's belief, experience or information. Reality can only ever be met head-on through present and direct firsthand contact. It is the difference between reading a dinner menu and mistaking the menu for the food compared to actually tasting the food itself. One is the information about something *(secondhand)*, the other is the actual experience of it *(firsthand)*.

Instead of living through the mind, you begin living from the heart: experiencing life immediately and directly rather than in a second hand way through the medium of thought. Simply realize that each thought is only an outside visitor that will soon leave if you do not cling to it and hold it hostage.

Practical Exercise: *Take a moment to sit quietly. Let mind come and go, let thoughts pass through freely without attaching to them. Watch thoughts come and go and just stay as you are.*

Be the witness to thought and imagination.

As you practice the exercise above, the mind will lose its power and fade into the background. Thoughts will become less attached to you and the mind will be relegated to the back seat, leaving **pure awareness** *(your true self)* in the driver's seat. Mind will take second place as the **heart** of your being will lead the way.

5 - The Thinker/Analyzer

You are not the analyzer, you are that which observes analyzing happening.

Thinking is a mechanism of the brain, used to problem solve and process information. Its job is to deconstruct, compartmentalize and process what it sees. When this is completed for anything other than that which is a practical task, over complication happens: resulting in confusion and the subsequent birth, or formation, of suffering.

Thinking cannot solve the issue of direct experience as it cannot allow you to come into contact with reality. The only way to truly understand yourself and reality is to experience it directly without the interference and distortion of thinking. You can only come to know reality through awareness and beingness, which is to say - **to go to the experience of being aware in this moment.** This is the tool which allows you to enter the immediate reality of existence **as it is** in the present.

Once we are able to observe the thought process and detach more, we will then be able to wake-up to a level of reality within ourselves that is vast, open, expansive and free. This then creates an inner reality that is free from the knots and tangles of compulsive thinking. We then become unbound from the limitations of the body-mind and transcend to a more expansive state of consciousness.

As the move from a contracted state of consciousness to a vast and open one occurs, it gives us the space to become aware of all the blocks that we have been experiencing - allowing us to realize that the internal suffering we were subject to came from what we '**believed**' and gave attention to within the mind.

Once we step out of the mental thought-codes and establish ourselves as the **observer** of our thoughts, we are freed in that very instant. The shift is an immediate one which transports us from '*thinker*' to '*conscious observer*'.

Spontaneous awakening happens when we see that we are not the thinker, but instead the one underneath the thinking.

Belief in being the thinker keeps the dream of the finite-self alive. However, when we consciously reunite with the Infinite-Self we discover that we are situated behind the thinker and not in the middle of it.

The key to being present in the moment is to take time to **STOP** completely: internally and externally at first, then just internally. The average mind never stops. Thinking is happening all day long, often because it is being fueled with the attention and fascination of personal identity (*belief in being the analyzer*).

One is constantly indulging and giving attention to thinking activity. So, when we say stop, it means to not only stop what you are doing physically, but to stop thinking for a moment. Stop engaging in thoughts and let them pass through the mind freely without identifying with them (*giving them your belief and attention*).

Practical Exercise: *For just a few moments, see if you can stop thinking. Then stop thinking once again for a few moments. Do this continually as a practice.*

We all have the power to completely stop internally and externally for a moment. We very simply stop all thinking for a moment, and then continue once again. We take a moment to not engage in thoughts, but instead to allow them clear passage to move through the mind untouched. If we do this continually we will experience deep peace as we break free from the pull of constant mind utterances. Eventually we will be able to stop internally whilst still moving and operating externally.

The thinking processes are an interesting phenomenon because the moment you begin to observe them closely… they start to disappear.

It is similar to clouds evaporating under the heat of a blisteringly hot sun on a summer's day. The clouds cannot survive in the intense heat, leaving the sky clear and blue. In the same way, thoughts cannot last under the watchfulness of an intense direct-awareness.

Try this practice now...

Practical Exercise: *Ask yourself, 'what thoughts are occupying my mind at this moment?'*

Allow this question to draw your attention towards what is happening in your mind right now and simply observe whatever thoughts or images are present at this moment. Do not judge or indulge in a mental debate about what is there.

Simply observe, with detachment, as though you are watching the mind from a distance. If thoughts are there great, if thoughts are not there then that's great too - just continue to watch whatever activity appears in the mind. Continue to do that for a while.

The more that you practice this exercise at intervals throughout the day and even when you are sat at home or lying in your bed, you will gradually begin to experience a greater capacity to disengage from the mind.

The more you are able to disengage from the mind, the more peace, joy, bliss and freedom you will feel. In the absence of mind activity, you experience the love of being. The trick here is to not allow the mind to pull you back into thinking when you are observing the thoughts in the mind *(although, in the beginning you may find that this does happen from time to time)*. Nevertheless, stay with it... as the more you do so, the more you will find that you can **'watch'** the mind for longer and longer periods without falling back into the **'thinking trap'**.

The real key here is to not allow yourself to become enmeshed in a struggle with your mind. Should you become enveloped in a tussle, it unfortunately means that you have slipped back into the thinking whirlpool of the mind once again - totally defeating the object of the exercise. We fall back into the mind as soon as we judge the mind. Do not judge... just witness.

Simply stay as a watcher.

Practical Exercise (Resting Concepts): *The next time the mind feels overwhelming or a mental dialogue or story is playing in the mind, just rest and relax all thinking for a couple of seconds. Whatever thoughts, stories or ideas are playing in the mind, just rest them.*

For a few moments, simply let go of all thoughts. Everyone has the power to do this. Take a deep breath, detach and give away all thoughts.

As you do this you may find a great silent space appear within you: feeling momentary rest and freedom from all stressful thinking. In this momentary gap, inner peace and freedom emerges. This silent space is not something that is created, but rather it is something that is uncovered. It has always been there, it's just that your attention on mind has been obscuring it.

You are not the mind, thoughts or the thinker. You are that which came **before** all thinking noise. You are that in which all thoughts and thinking are taking place in the view of.

Realize the Self that is beyond mind and you automatically transport yourself from the direct experience of the finite to the Infinite.

6 - Losing the Plot

All that stands between you and reality is a personal script.

All suffering, turmoil and self-limitation arrives from the belief of being an *'apart identity'* (separate being) from the rest of life and living through a mental story based on this *'apart identity'*.

In other words – *If you think you are a someone-*
...going somewhere... trying to get something... that is
going to amount to something, suffering will become
the result.

If you think you are a **'someone'**, it means you have a
personal identity that is naturally and inherently in
opposition to life - whether you are consciously or
subconsciously aware of it or not. If one has the **root
sense** that they are a separate entity, they will always
stand in opposition to life in order to maintain their
own independent survival above all else. They will
always seek to protect and keep their identity in place -
which will result in attachment through fear.

If you have a **need** to get **'somewhere'**, then it means
that you are not in alignment with your **present
fulfillment** because you are trying to seek your
fulfillment in the future. Within your direct experience
it splits you in two, thus creating an inner conflict
within you. The real part of you is already fulfilled and
present in the moment while the conditioned-self is
searching for fulfillment in the future. The latter is the
illusion which keeps you restless, never allowing you
to enjoy yourself in the present reality.

By trying to get **'something'**, you are saying that you
are in a state of **'lack'** and need something from the
external to make you happy and complete. In this way
you are fundamentally saying that you are not enough
and that you need more to be happy and at peace.

This means that you **lean** on external objects and circumstances to be fulfilled, and this fulfillment is always dependent on the world of **transient things**. What this means is that the things that you try to acquire and hold, will always slip through your fingers like sand. In other words, you will never be truly happy and fulfilled, and therefore you will always experience emptiness and sadness as a result.

This means you will never feel complete, because you will always have a hole inside you that can never stay filled for any length of time.

And finally, wanting things to *'amount'* to something shows that your hope of **salvation** is firmly rooted **only** in the result of something coming true in the future. This means that if it doesn't happen you will become sad and disappointed and therefore will suffer.

If it does come true you will be happy for a while and will then become **dissatisfied** again and will seek to chase the next thing. You will also become restless whilst in the pursuit of needing a particular outcome to happen. In all scenarios you will inevitably suffer for the illusion of thinking that you need a result to be happy and complete.

If you wake up beyond all of these misperceptions you will discover a lasting fulfillment and satisfaction that you have never felt before *(maybe only when you were a child have you felt something similar)*. This innate happiness comes from the awakening of the **hereness state**. It is a natural sense of completion and satisfaction that comes from the freedom and joy that is experienced in the **now** reality.

What ties the illusion together and keeps it in circulation is the belief in a story, in a psychological plotline in the head. One must lose this plot to be free from self-created suffering. If you lose the plot you lose time, if you lose time you awaken to the timeless dimension, and from the timeless dimension true reality becomes known and your **true Infinite-Self** shines through brightly.

The finite-self thrives by living through a personal story, a story that exists in a perception of time. The story is an accumulation of past experiences carried through to the present moment. This mental storyline is a dialogue that keeps one rooted in the head, it distorts reality when we believe the story to be real. The story is a thought based projection that is superimposed onto the present reality, people and life circumstances.

It is like wearing a pair of red tinted spectacles and then believing the whole world is red. As soon as you take the spectacles off, you soon see reality in its bare state and realize it wasn't red after all! Nor was it ever!

Become aware of the stories that are most regularly played in your mind, maybe a story of not being worthy, of being a failure, or not being good enough. Or maybe a story of being depressed, scared, anxious or stressed. Or perhaps it is a story about your external life circumstances.

Become aware of these mental scripts and see that you are only the one perceiving them. They come and go.

What are these beliefs which run as stories and sentences in your mind? A sentence believed becomes a life sentence: it becomes your life sentence. If you believe the sentence of the mind...then it becomes your daily living experience. How convincing they can seem: *'he hurt me'*, or *'I am a bad person'*. Observe how the story tries to grip you just like a movie at the cinema does. No matter how real it may seem, can you see it is just a false meaning created by your mind?

When you go watch a movie, you know it's not real, you know it's just a show, but even so you sometimes get lost in the drama of it. So too happens with your mind. Take a step back and be the **spectator** of the mental plotline. Don't take it too seriously...it is only the echoes of collected information from the past.

Your deeper nature is that of the spectator not the spectacle before you. Claiming to be the spectacle is an illusion which brings a heavy cost, the cost is suffering.

Practical Exercise: *Whenever the next plotline and sentencing runs through your mind... become intensely aware of it and ask the question* **'Am I really this story or the one watching it'?**

A mental script can only exist with time. There can be no script when you are in the direct experience of the here and now because the moment the script plays in the mind it has already become past - and past is not real it is just a thought. Only the **immortal present moment** is real and true, and that is right where you are.

All mentally scripted stories are birthed from the past. Let the story go, along with the past and just be presently aware of the here and now.

When you do, a whole new world of possibilities becomes known. The **now** is the point of Infinite possibilities and the Infinite-Self. Relax the story and enter the true reality of hereness.

7 - Feelings and Emotions

All emotions, sprouted first from a thought which was believed.

Emotions are a product of something that we have thought or believed beforehand to be true. If we think it and believe it then the body begins to excrete certain chemicals into our system, which produces our feelings or emotions.

A feeling is often something that can linger under the surface for many hours, sort of in the background of our consciousness, whereas an emotion is more of a shorter quicker burst of energy rising to the surface instantaneously. Just to know this is a very good thing, because we can then begin to become aware of these functions of the body-mind system, and just being aware of this already creates some distance and freedom from them.

Often when we have certain emotions or feelings, a conceptual story can become attached to it. The story will often perpetuate the feeling or emotion and give it more energy to make it stronger.

For instance, the mind will firstly label the feeling or emotion as being good or bad. This then sets the precedent for the story thereafter being either a positive or negative one, and thus determining how you feel.

It may say 'I feel terrible today', and so with that story comes along a reinforcement of that feeling. It can be a vicious cycle where the thought feeds the feeling and the feeling once again feeds more thoughts. It can soon snowball into a downward spiral of unpleasantness and inner suffering.

We can stop this snowball effect dead in its tracks by doing the practice of not classifying the feeling or emotion as being **good/bad** or **positive/negative**. Instead we just look at them in an unbiased way, and we simply continue to observe them with a **pure silent watchfulness**.

This then stops the sensation from snowballing and allows it to eventually pass, because no emotion can be kept alive without having the energy of identity behind it. No sensation, feeling or emotion can last forever: they are very fleeting and changeable phenomena's, and so they will eventually fade and depart if we don't continue to feed them with a mental story.

Practical Exercise: We can do a daily practice of checking in with our feelings and emotions in the body at any time by asking the question *'What is occurring inside the body at this moment?*

This is a question that directs our awareness inside towards whatever feelings or emotions may be lingering in the body in that instant.

This spotlights what is happening in the body, and through the subtle **watching** of these phenomena in the body we already begin to create some distance from them, thus freeing ourselves from their grip. In fact, through a **silent nonjudgmental watchfulness** of the feeling or emotion, we create a gap of **space** between us as pure awareness and the arising phenomena of a feeling or emotion occurring in the body.

If we stay as the watcher, we will find that the emotion or feeling begins to dissipate and loses its authority over us.

Whilst observing the feeling or emotion we will see that - *there is the feeling or emotion* - and here I am as the observer of it. In other words, we see that those bodily phenomena are not who we really are – instead, we are the one watching it! The watcher was there before the emotion arose and it is there when the emotion leaves also.

This is a huge basis for inner freedom and tranquility, because unless we create some distance between the essential Self that we are and the body, we will always be a slave to the body's compulsions, thus suffering its changes. In this instance, compulsive emotions are one of the factors we can free ourselves from. We do this when we are the pure witness of our internal circumstance.

Section 2
Awakening Through Conscious Practice & Meditation

8 - The Nature of Authentic Meditation and Attention Meditation

Often in the beginning of awakening the subtle effort of attention is needed, in the end awareness alone will suffice.

Attention Meditation

What is the difference between attention meditation and authentic meditation?

Attention meditation is simply the concentration and focus of your awareness into a certain direction. Attention requires some effort as it is an initiated action. Effort may be needed to remove oneself from unconscious tendencies.

Authentic meditation is different, it is a subtle effortless noticing from our awareness, and it is simply the ability to consciously sense all that comes into our direct experience. We will speak more about awareness in a moment.

When most people start-out on the spiritual path or the path of awakening, much attention and effort is often required to break the habit and the heavy '*pull*' of the minds constant thinking.

Sometimes the mind has such a huge *'pull'* and is so busy that it requires some training of attention and lessening of the minds load to create enough space to allow the subtlety of awareness to shine through.

When engaging in attention meditation as laid out below, it is important to start out with close attention to each practice, not excessive effort, but enough effort to purposely draw our attention in a particular direction. The attention needs to be trained to resist the old reactive forces and habits and to be cultivated to focus on the present moment and the beingness.

The Body

By becoming more aware of our body, an immediate shift can take place. This shift moves our attention from being lost in thinking and concentrates it more into our bodies. If you fully concentrate on your foot or both feet for instance, it is almost impossible to have full attention of your feet whilst at the same time being lost in your thoughts. If for example, you focus one hundred percent of your attention on one of your feet and the sensations therein, notice how the mind seems to subside as two things cannot have your **full** attention simultaneously. Please try that now...

Do this with any part of the body and you will find thinking subsides as you are no longer feeding it with your attention.

Breathing

If there is one thing we can rely upon to always be here whilst we are present in this body, it is the constant movement caused by our breathing reflex. The breath is the very thing that ties us to the body itself, as without it we would immediately leave the body. So because the activity of the breath is always present, we can very easily use it as a point of focus for attention meditation. The very second we start to pay attention of the breath and its movement, we automatically start to become more aware and present.

Breathing more fully and consciously can have a huge effect on ones level of awareness in daily living. As you take more oxygen in and become present as you do so, your whole body, mind and awareness will become more relaxed, clear and enhanced. You will feel more alive and aware. The practice below is a way to take control of the breath and therefore the mind, as the mind and breath are intimately connected. If you breathe slowly and deeply... you will also slow down the mental chatter.

Practical Exercise: (The Breath of Stillness)

Pay attention to the breath and breathe more fully...

Focus on how your stomach and chest rises and falls with each inhalation and exhalation of the breath.

Simply take a moment to breathe consciously and pay attention to the silent pauses between each breath as you hold the breath in and out between each inhale and exhale...

Concentrate on the air as it passes in through your nostrils on the in-breath and how the air passes your lips or nostrils on the out-breath...

Each time you breathe out, allow your body to relax more and more. Allow yourself to drop into the silent stillness and watch and feel the breath and gaps of no-breath for a couple of minutes...

The Five Senses

Lose your mind and come to your senses.

We have five senses of the body: smell, taste, touch, sight and hearing and when we pay full attention to our senses, our direct experience of life becomes greatly magnified. It is like switching the volume up on our life experience. So a great way to be **here** in the **now** and divert focus away from thinking, is to pay total attention to your senses.

Start to pay more attention to the various sounds in

your room, like the clock ticking or the cars passing by outside. Or you can simply go and listen to the sounds of nature; listen to the wind blowing through the leaves and the birds singing.

As you are reading this book, become aware of how the book feels in your hands, how it feels upon your skin. Avoid the tendency to mentally describe it and instead just feel it... sense it.

Next time you sit down to eat, make yourself extremely attentive of each mouthful of food you chew. See if you can eat more slowly and savor each bite, whilst enjoying all of the flavors and textures of each mouthful. Wherever you are, start to focus more closely on the vibrancy of colors and how certain objects stand out from their background. Notice the many different shades of color. See how your richness of sight improves with this practice, see how your whole sight becomes enhanced. Simply observe without mental discrimination of what is seen.

Lastly, pay attention to your sense of smell. See if you can savor the smell of a fresh cut lawn, or the smell of a beautiful perfume. The more attentive you are to the smells around you, the less you will be in the head.

Practical Exercise: *Become a 'walking, talking sensory organ,' experience life in every moment through your senses and not through the mind.*

As you do this you will find that the body becomes your primary present experience instead of the mind.

As you begin to practice meditation and paying attention to the here and now, start with attention first. Attention means that you are making an initial effort to disengage from thinking and instead placing attention on something else in particular, which is often needed in the beginning.

As your practice continues, see if you can become more subtle in your meditation and move away from a focused attention and instead towards a lighter more relaxed awareness.

9 - Authentic Meditation

Authentic meditation includes only one main ingredient- ...awareness.

Whatever awareness becomes aware of, is meditation.
Whatever you do with awareness is meditation.
Silent Awareness without thought is the be all and end all, of real authentic meditation.

Just Silent Awareness

Awareness just is. It need not be forced or cultivated, and it **just is what it is**... always present... never disappearing or appearing... it is always there and remains there even when the disappearing and appearing things are witnessed by it.

Awareness is always silently there just as the stars are always there whether it is night or day. So when we speak of being aware, you should know that you are always aware. If you were not aware... you would not be able to read these words or experience anything of any kind. Awareness is the only essential ingredient of all experiencing, because everything must report to it. Don't take my word for it... check it out yourself now. Can you have any experience of any kind without the gaze of awareness being there to notice it?

Can you at this moment be aware of who it is that is being aware?

So when we speak of becoming more aware, it's not that we should try to cultivate more awareness... because you are always aware, it just simply means that we should become conscious of awareness. Just simply notice this.

Be aware that you are aware.

This is what it means to 'become' more aware.

It is a case of consistently recognizing awareness.

Practical Exercise - Try these three exercises:

Try to not be aware right now...

Turn awareness on itself...

Become aware of awareness itself...

Most people become so lost in the busy mind and the external world that they simply forget awareness, or they 'think' they are aware and take this for granted and so never turn awareness on itself. This means that people operate unconsciously most of the time. In other words, they overlook awareness. It becomes like a precious object that is locked away in a box and forgotten. Strictly speaking, it is not appreciated or noticed and the consequence of this is that what we ignore diminishes within our experience.

When awareness goes unnoticed, its expansiveness in terms of how it is experienced... depletes greatly. It is like having a consciousness that has the potential to be as expansive and panoramic as a cinema screen- ...but instead it's only achieving the range of a small mobile phone screen. Imagine the difference of experience through each perception? One would feel very constricted and limited, while the other would be light and free. The first is like having the volume turned down in life as opposed to having the volume cranked up to maximum. Maximum volume means a maximum experience of life. One is dull and the other is full of richness. Which would you choose?

If you have a small range of consciousness, you will only experience a small range of life. If however you have a large range of consciousness, then all of a sudden the whole universe can be accessed and perceived by you. So the key to increasing your entire experience of life lies in the quality of your awareness, and that starts by being more and more aware from present moment to present moment.

This is what true authentic meditation is, simply being aware... just noticing... without any thought or judgement.

So everywhere you go and everything you do can become your meditation practice.

Eating your breakfast in the morning if done with full awareness becomes meditation, or driving to work if done with total awareness turns into meditation, washing the dishes or ironing, showering or cleaning- ...everything can become your meditation. This is what it means to awaken to the true self in daily life: allow everything to be your **meditation**.

In this way your whole life will blossom in ways you could have never imagined. You will become incredibly happy and joyful. Your life will turn to riches and gold through the enhanced quality and bliss of your everyday experience. You will become much more intelligent and present in situations and especially with people. As a consequence of this, even the things you do in the world will improve, because more awareness means more quality in what you do, and more aware-ness means more **aliveness!**

The foundation of your daily meditation practice for awakening and enlightenment is simply this: just bring a greater awareness and sense of nowness into everyday living. Nowness means to just be in the moment with the totality of your being, and to be fully watchful and alert in each instance.

10 - Being Aware Here Now

The door to reality opens by being aware of what is now.

If Spiritual Enlightenment or Self-Realization could be summed up in one phrase, it would be this: *'Be aware here now'*. That is essentially all that is needed.
If you are one hundred percent consciously aware here and now without unconsciousness (*which means to be lost in thinking*) and continue as such, then you are Enlightened. True Enlightenment is a phenomena that is paradoxically both simple but extremely profound.

It means that you have gone from the world of the finite into the true world of the Infinite. This can never ultimately be explained from the outside looking in. It can only be directly experienced and known from the inside looking out.

Enlightenment is not about having great intellectual knowledge and heaps of ideas and concepts. If that were the case...then a large portion the world would be considered Enlightened. No, Enlightenment fundamentally means...to be totally awake from the unconscious dream of thinking, that's it.

When you are no longer identified with the body/mind mechanism (*finite self*), then you are completely free as the Infinite-Self. You go from **body** to **being**, and being is eternal. Being is the energy of the Infinite.

Hereness

The sense of being present is the experience of hereness.

Now is the only moment there ever is. It is ever present and forever here. Time in the form of yesterday and tomorrow is an illusion created only by thinking. When we stop thinking we realize only the timeless reality is real and true. **Hereness** refers to consciously being here in the present moment, as the moment itself. To be one with the moment and have a sense of timelessness can be described as the state of hereness.

This moment right here as the now moment is inescapable. It is immovable, it cannot be avoided.

Practical Exercise: Try your very best to not be here right now...Did you succeed?

As you just found out, it is impossible to escape it. This is good news. It means that you are in fact, always here now in the present. Your body is here now and even your awareness is here now. The only thing that *'appears'* to not be here now...is thought. But then, even a thought can only happen now.

The only reason that it appears you are not in the moment, is because you have allowed your attention to be dazzled by the bright lights of memories and imagination in your mind – all of which, can seem very convincing as if they are actually happening in time. But in actuality, all thinking only takes place here and now. Everything is only existing in **timelessness**.

If you could look at yourself from outside your body, and watch yourself thinking, you would see that thinking is only happening **now**, it cannot happen anywhere else. Those thoughts running through the head can only occur now along with everything else, and that is because time does not really exist, only the present is real.

Even though all thoughts are also only occurring in the present, the experience of them through identification gives the **thinker** an illusory sense of time. Once we begin to create some distance from thinking by seeing that we are the one **witnessing** the thoughts and are not the thoughts themselves, we step out of the perception of time and start to see that everything including all thought-phenomena - is simultaneously happening in the now.

Awakening cannot occur in the future, as the future does not exist, and so awakening can only ever happen now. Not tomorrow, not next week or next year... but now. Only here and only now. The experience of awakening can only happen in the present reality. The finite identity would like it to take time because that means it can survive indefinitely-...because the future will never come. This gives the mind time to put it off and continue its dominance. Unfortunately for the mind and luckily for you, awakening can only happen **now** in your immediate experience. So drop the idea of time and awaken here and now.

Drop all past and future ideas and just be here now. Many beings find themselves burdened by the past with guilt or shame and have fear and anxiety about the future. This keeps them in a perception of time which keeps them in suffering and self-limitation.

What one must come to realize is that we are not responsible for all of our past actions. Rather, we were being led by the unconsciousness of the programmed mind and our conditioned biology. We have all been in a deep slumber sleep walking our way through life.

Once you awaken beyond mind you will see that everything you have done unto this point has been led by unconscious forces that you believed to be you. Let go of the past and future and you will find the **everlasting life** of the sacred now moment. This is the way to clear all past mistakes, all future fears and discover liberation.

Start to let go of the past and future by ceasing to ask the questions of *'Why?'* and *'Where?'* The conditioned - self is always living through the past and seeking to carry it into the future, therefore ignoring the present. One of the main ways in which the conditioned self keeps the past alive is by always asking the question *'Why?'* It says *'Why did this happen?'* *(Referring to a past event)* and by asking the question it ties you down to the past, because it is a question that can never ultimately be answered.

There are no ultimate answers to why certain things happen in life. The reason for this is that there is no real reason. Life just happens and no intellectual answer of why something happens will suffice. Life is much more mysterious than that. We cannot see the bigger picture of countless events: one event leads to the next continuously forever, and where does it end? To understand why something happened, you would have to know the end result of it, but how can you know the end result when there isn't an end? In other words, how can you define something based on Infinity?

Each event is just a sequence of events occurring now and leading into eternity, and eternity is always now... now... now.

The same is true for the question of 'Where?' (*Referring to a potential future direction*). Asking this question makes you focus on the future, because when you ask **'Where are things headed?'** you are saying that **now** is not sufficient enough and that the future has more of your attention. It means that you are seeking to work out where things are leading to, and you do this because you think that the future will bring you something better.

By engaging in this, we are basically saying - whether we are consciously aware of it or not - that the reality of ourselves in the present is not enough. It means that we are valuing fantasy and illusion over reality. One is the real and the other is the unreal, one leads to suffering and the other to freedom. Both questions keep us lost in a sense of time through **confusion** and **hope**. Confusion of why something happened in the past and the hopes of something better appearing in the future. Each time-based-focus takes your sense of eternal presence away. Your experience becomes one of being trapped in time: guilt and regret of the past and fear and hope of the future.

Practical Exercise: Whatever events happen... *never ask the questions of* **'Why?'** *and* **'Where?'** *This will free you from the mental suffering that is caused by* **confusion** *and* **stressful thoughts.**

Notice how these questions will continually be asked by the mind through habit? Pay them no attention and realize the truth: the truth being that there is no true sufficient answer or meaning you will find to these questions. There are no definitive answers you will find. Any answer would only be a speculation that keeps you preoccupied in a sense of time. Instead, be here now and experience the mystery and wonder of life.

When you relax the need to know... you will find yourself in the flow...

Stay in the flow of life by being **conscious** of your **direct experience** in the **present.**

One way in which we can bring ourselves back to noticing our current experience in present moment, is to ask the question:

'When am I?'

Ask this question throughout the day as a reminder to bring your **awareness** back to the **experience** of **hereness**.

Do you reside in the past, future or present?

Resist the urge of the mind to want to answer the question intellectually, as this will do no good. We are not seeking an answer. The true answer is in the experience of being present in the **Eternal Now**. Allow the question to bring you to the **direct experience** of hereness by way of reminding you of what is real and true.

You come to the truth not by believing the question or by saying '*now*', but through the process of self-investigation initiated by the question. Self-investigation is the means of looking and checking out our immediate experience. Allow the question to act as a pointer towards what is true in this moment.

Nowness

Now is all there is... if you will just notice it.

Nowness refers to the awareness of being in the here-now reality, of what is here and present in this moment. When you notice this immediate moment, you begin to align with it, because now you are no longer in the head and are instead looking from the position of awareness, and awareness is always one with the here and now moment.

When you start to relax and become attentively aware of this moment, you step into an open state of **nowness**: your **original** state. From this original state all the pleasant qualities of peace, joy and happiness are felt, including a sense of gratitude and reverence for this moment. We start to see that life is now, has always been now and will always be now. We start to enter reality consciously and leave behind the foggy illusion of a thought-identity in a perception of time, and instead find the timeless reality all around us and within us.

To allow ourselves the experience of being here now without any expectation of anything else is a truly satisfying feeling. We begin to enjoy the present moment immensely. Consciously remind yourself of the constant nature of the here and now moment.

Practical Exercise: *Breathing in, 'I am aware of the present', breathing out, 'I am only here and now'.*

Allow the words to lead your awareness consciously into the present moment. Remember, nowness or hereness or any other word are just pointers towards the direct experience of what is here. Do not get stuck on the words. Instead, go to where they lead.

Another way to practice being aware of the moment is to focus on the things existing within it. What often happens is that we let ourselves get so *'fenced-in'* by paying attention to the mind, that we miss all the beauty and wonder around us...

One of the reasons that people often fail to pay true attention to the present moment, is that they *'think'* they know everything about it, and so give it very little notice and overlook it. But one of the beautiful things about awakening beyond the level of thought is that we soon see that what we *'thought'* we knew is not actually true. That beyond the mind the whole of existence returns to the beautiful mystery it once was when we were a child. The innocence of life returns to cradle us in its bosom.

When we don't know who we truly are, all learnt information can only become taught-ignorance - only serving to block us from making contact with true reality. In taught-ignorance we think we know when in fact, we do not. This becomes seen when we meet reality for the very first time. This first meeting of reality is what is termed as awakening. Awakening is our first introduction to the truth, and from that glimpse the thread of illusion quickly unravels.

We begin to see things and objects as if seeing them for the very first time. Life begins to take on a new freshness, and from this freshness we start to pay closer attention to everything around us in the here and now. Suddenly life... for the very first time... really comes to **life!**

Practical Exercise: To become aware of the moment:

Wherever you are, pay attention to the objects that surround you. For example, pay attention to a tree and the shape of the tree and its color and texture.

Look at the tree (or any object) as if seeing it for the very first time.

*Pick any object and observe it with the utmost interest and wonder. You can say, '**I know not what I see**'.*

By saying this we drop the minds previous information of the object and access the ability to see it as if for the first time once again.

Live and approach each moment like seeing it for the very first time. Each moment is fresh and brand new. Find the mystery of it.

Live here on earth as if you are the first and last being here. Approach all objects like you are encountering them for the very first time, and as if you may never see them again.

The Vibrant Aliveness of Being

*There is an animated essence within you that is truer to your real nature. This essence is the **life force energy.***

Within you at this moment is a tremendous **aliveness**, a beingness that is vibrant and totally present.

This vibrant alive beingness is a **pristine immortal life force energy** that is at our deepest core. When we occupy it consciously through our sense and feeling of it, it comes alive in us as a state of **pure presence** *(present being)*.

This presence is the state of natural alive energy within us at the *'being-level'* of our nature. This **being- level** is beyond that of the body and mind. It stretches past the mortal to the immortal essence of who we really are. It stretches past the body, but yet at the same time it is the very force that animates the body.

Our bodies are always in the immediate moment - which means that we can use the body like a rock or lead weight to ground us experientially in a state of hereness.

The body is always with us everywhere we go, and so it is something that we can depend upon as a point of awareness to bring us back down to the ground of the now moment.

This alive beingness is an energetic feeling within the whole body. It is a sense of presence that if felt fully brings an amazingly fulfilling feeling to us: a sense of being whole and complete, of being content and **tranquil** in the now. To presently experience our whole body and being in this moment without thought or judgement, but instead experientially, is a truly **blissful** affair.

As we become more in contact with the being-level of who we really are, we will find ourselves evermore present, alive and wakeful. This life force energy is the true animating principle of all life, and it exists within you right now, as us. When we relax into this being-level of who we really are, all stress melts away, and what we are left with is a pure and complete sense of present-vibrant- alive-existence.

Practical Exercise: To notice our natural sense of being:

Breathing in, 'I'm aware of my whole body.'
Breathing out, 'I'm aware of my whole body.'

Quite simply, as we breathe in we become aware of our whole body in that moment, and as we breathe out we again become aware of the whole body.

If we wish, we can say these words either in our mind

or out loud as a mantra, which reminds us to breathe and become aware of the entire body. Allow the words to be a reminder for you to pay attention to the whole body and to feel it fully. If we do this throughout the day at intervals, it will dramatically increase our level of self-awareness and our noticing of the present moment. You and the present moment will come alive!

One thing that is innate in all human beings is the natural sense of existence. It is the joy and tranquility of being: the simple but profound sense of existing. It's the natural sense of *'I exist'*, the most primal and foundational sense of being here in the present. It is to simply experience a sense of aliveness to its absolute maximum without diversion from thoughts that want to take our attention elsewhere. It is an indescribably beautiful direct experience to encounter, and it is here right now for the taking... if we would only come to notice it. Notice this sense of existence and aliveness here and now.

Practical Exercise: That you can do anywhere at any time:

Breathing in, 'I feel alive'
Breathing out, 'I sense I exist'

Do not 'think' about existence or even your existence, instead use your senses and perception to become aware. Can you sense it and feel it? Can you feel the aliveness within each cell of your body? Can you feel the vibrant life force energy within?

When you sense this aliveness within, it removes your awareness from thinking and plants it firmly within the foundations of the body. When you are in the body and not lost in the mind, you become more attentive to the nowness of the moment.

Whenever you become lost in the mind and you are immersed in stressful thoughts, bring your awareness to the feeling of *'aliveness'* within you. It is a pleasant feeling that is the most basic sense of existence a being has. It is the sense you get of *'I exist'*, the feeling of existing and being alive. Before the formation of mental concepts such as *'I am* this' or 'I am that' came, there was just a feeling of **I AM**: a strong, present, sense of being. Whenever you sense it, you will break out of the dream of thought and come back to yourself, becoming centered and grounded in the moment.

Life is full of the **joy of being**, the joy of being yourself right now, surrounded by beautifully colored objects, sounds, smells and sensations. Life is a rich tapestry of experiences waiting to be enjoyed in the present. This moment is the only place that life can ever exist, and if you are not here consciously...paying attention to it, but are instead living in your head, then you are missing reality and life. Life will seem to pass you by, feeling as though you have never really been here, as if you have never fully lived consciously, all because you have been lost in an illusionary perception of time in the realm of mind. This is the greatest tragedy anyone could ever experience. To walk through life in an unconscious way is a waste of your precious life experience.

Awaken to reality as it is now and you will awaken to everlasting life, and to treasures beyond description.

Another powerful question we can ask ourselves to awaken us to the nowness of life is:

'What is here?'

The question **'What is here?'** is a question that is asking us to directly experience what is here in this now moment. It is pointing us towards noticing what is contained in this moment. It is to see objects and sounds **'just as they are'** without filtering it through the mind, and without labeling. It is to feel our bodies and to be aware of our natural sense of existence. It is asking *'Can you be aware and directly experience everything in this moment without an ounce of unconsciousness?'*

So allow this question to do its work by asking it whenever you forget to be conscious of the present moment, and it will bring you back to being aware of the here and now and your sense of aliveness within it. Nowness, or the quality of being here now is the doorway to freedom and Enlightenment.

The Quietness of Being

Underneath the noise of the body-mind there is a silent intelligent presence.

The periphery of your body is just like clouds moving across the sky: clouds of thoughts, feelings and sensations. In the same way as the sky holds clouds, below the surface of the body, there is an immovable depth that remains calm and still - always unaffected by the unsteadiness of the constantly changing occurrences happening within it. This is the **Quietness of Being**.

This quietness of being is a stillness of calm and tranquility that is at the base and foundation of your most intimate core nature.

Stillness is as it implies: a place of inner still. To be **'still'**, means the absence of any inner movement. It is where we withdraw from the mind and senses and enter into the natural place of calm and silence within. A place where no activity is present, only the effortless silent witnessing of activity remains.

It is the place within us that is beneath the activities of the body and mind, just as the depths of the ocean are completely motionless despite the extreme motion of the waves above. Stillness occurs when we slip into this place beneath what is being thought, believed and felt in the moment. It is a timeless and deep dimension of Intelligence within, which can only be experienced in the moment.

One way that we can get in touch with this stillness is to listen to the silence within and all around us. To listen to this silence as often as possible is a beautiful exercise that takes us deeper into its possibilities.

Listen to the pure silence within a quiet room. Notice the silence in between each tick of the clock. Notice the silence prior to a car passing outside your window and as silence returns… once the car has disappeared.

Practical Exercise: *When next in a noisy environment, listen to all the different noises and note from where these noises appear… and to where they disappear…*

All sound appears from silence and descends back into silence. Notice this and hear this…

Can you hear the soundless sound in between sounds? Contemplate this…

We can also pay attention to the silence in between

words and thoughts as we speak. Be aware of your silent spaces and pauses in-between your words...

As you listen to others be aware of the silent spaces in their speech. As you think... observe any quiet gaps... no matter how tiny... in between each thought and see if you can notice from where each thought arises and to where each thought disappears. Notice this.

Anytime we become aware of silence it is an opportunity to become very still within and connect with our true nature beyond the mind. This silence and stillness may also be witnessed through being conscious of our breathing.

Practical Exercise: *Notice the stillness in the moment of gently holding the breath in between the inhalation and exhalation. Notice the quietness at the end of each **in** and **out** breath. Take a moment to be aware of it now.*

The thinking mind and breathing are very much connected. When our minds are erratic and busy our breathing often becomes short and fast, but when our minds are extremely relaxed and calm our breathing becomes slow and deep. When we breathe in for a moment and stop whilst holding it... our minds will stop also. Please check this out and experience it yourself.

Practical Exercise: *Take the time to notice how slow or fast your mind and breath is at this moment and see if they match...*

Now breathe in and out three times, with long slow deep breaths. Then take a deep breath and gently hold it... Make sure to relax your body as you do so...

As you hold the breath in, turn your attention towards the thinking mind. Notice what thoughts are in the mind... if any... and just be aware of them without judgement...

As you hold your breath in, become aware and look for the spaces of silence within... Allow yourself to rest within these silent spaces...

Use this daily technique as often as possible to establish contact with the silence within you in the now moment.

Make silence your friend and it will reward you with the gift of a tranquil state of being... in its entirety... depth and fullness.

The Supreme Witnessing Intelligence

Like the reflection in the mirror being witnessed... so too are you.

In the middle of all experiences there is an ever present **supreme witnessing** taking place. To have any experience, and I invite you to look at this now as you are reading these words, there must be an element of something that is conscious of the experience. Something that is aware and watchful of the experience. For instance, something that is aware of reading taking place right now. Who or what is watchful of this reading that is happening?

Without that watchful element there can be no way to have an experience. There can be no way to experience anything nor report upon an experience.

And so, in the midst of all experiences, there is a watchfulness which is present. It is a supreme watching, of which it itself, is not involved in the activity of what it is watching. It is like being perched upon a high mountain and being able to see the vast view for hundreds of miles around. You are observing from such a great spaciousness, which would not be able to be seen, if you were situated down in the valley. Down in the valley you would not be able to see the woods for the trees!

It is like sitting at the side of a busy road and watching the cars whiz by. You are watching them, but you are not whizzing by with them. You are not moving as they move, you do not go as they go, it's like you're at a distance watching the activity without being the activity itself.

This supreme watching is apart from whatever phenomena it watches, and so in this way it is free from whatever it views, because whatever it sees will eventually pass by while the seer of it will stay there after it is gone, and will still be watching. This supreme witnessing is a viewer of all thoughts, feelings, emotions, situations and circumstances. It is able to observe all passing phenomena in the constantly changing world of form and appearance.

In our true witnessing nature, we can see that we are not the appearances of the world but that our true identity is far beyond that. Paradoxically, we see that we are not the things of the world but yet at the same time that we exist **in** and **as** the source of all things.

This witnessing is static. It does not budge, and it remains as it is regardless of whatever experiences pass before it. It has been there throughout all of the experiences you have ever had. From when you were a child, to when you were a teenager, to being an adult. It is there right now reading these words. This supreme witnessing is our true self. It is the core of who we essentially are beyond the body-mind and so called material world. This paradox comes into our direct experience as we begin to transcend the body-mind and move towards the nonphysical witness.

Practical Exercise: *Right now go ahead and witness whatever thoughts are appearing in the mind.*

Stay as a **silent witness** to the thoughts without thinking about what you are witnessing. If you think or judge the thoughts that you witness, then it means you have succumbed to the mind and are no longer in the position of the Supreme Infinite witness, but rather, situated once again in the thinking-mind and finite identity.

If you witness a thought, and then are having resisting thoughts about the thought you just witnessed, it means you are remembering a thought that has now already passed. In other words, you are suffering because of inner resistance towards a thought that is now long gone. This is the subtly of mind. Just stay an impartial witness to all thoughts equally.

Just silently witness the thoughts without get involved in the thoughts, which means not to think about the thoughts. However, if you find that thinking about the thoughts has taken over, then simply witness those thoughts also. If you wander off into thinking... become aware you have done so and very gently return as the witness of those thoughts. Each time we do this, we get further and further back behind and underneath the mind so to speak. As thoughts disappear in our witnessing, a greater peace and expansion becomes known to us. The more we witness thoughts the more and more thoughts begin to melt away and leave us clean and pure. Our perception becomes clear and pristine - like a freshly washed mirror.

So when we return back to this supreme witnessing we find and discover that we are actually completely free from the phenomenal world of the changing. This is because **it's impossible to fully watch thinking and think at the same time.** You can't do both, and so the quality of total watchfulness will automatically mean that you have disengaged from all thinking movements instantly. Try it.

When you are not watchful, the unconsciousness of thinking occurs and takes back over. However when you are very watchful you become completely conscious of your present experience and naturally disengage from thought. Freedom from the mind means freedom from suffering and the revealing of truth.

So as we begin to very consciously become aware of this watchfulness, in a sense **watching the watchfulness**, we start to create more distance and space between the watchfulness that we are and the mind phenomena. One of the most beautiful ways of doing this is to start and witness the **thought-codes** going on in the head. For most people, their watchfulness is so heavily identified and engrossed with the thought-codes, that there does not seem to be any gap or space there. It feels as though they are the mind!

This is why most people say 'I am my thinking' or 'I am my thoughts', but if we look closely we can see that there is a witnessing of the thoughts taking place, in which the thoughts are certainly appearing in front of, and *'in'* the witnessing itself.

Please check for yourself now and find your position in relation to the thoughts...

Are you in front of thoughts, behind them... underneath them or in the middle of them? This is very important.

Whatever you can watch must surely be in front of you, no...? Please look and see...

As we start to become aware of this and find where we are looking from, and very consciously begin to look from this supreme witnessing, we inevitably begin to create a gap between what we essentially are and the phenomenal world, which is that of thoughts, feelings, emotions, circumstance and events.

As we create more of a gap from the mind, there is a boundlessness that develops, in which we find so much spaciousness present. In that spacious-ness we find freedom from the turbulence of mind noise and worldly phenomena. Space is the gateway in which we connect to our pure essence, and that essence cannot be harmed. In that space we break free from the confines of the body and mind.

Naturally, being in this place of supreme witnessing, which is not actually involved in the constant activity and change of the occurring world brings an immense freedom, peace and joy to our present experience. Even extreme bliss and ecstasy can emerge whilst in the position of this supreme witnessing.

We can start to develop space by being in each moment: totally watchful and conscious of the thoughts going through our head and to witness the psychological script that is playing in the mind. It is a storyline of thoughts acting as a running commentary of events.

For most people there is a constant internal dialogue playing in their heads, and many think that this is who they are. They think the mental story is true and give it their belief. But if you simply become an observer without engaging or indulging in any story – or in thinking, a gap will start to develop and you will see that, in a sense, you are detached from the thinking. You will discover there is a space between what you essentially are as this supreme witnessing and the thinking itself.

There is so much space there. In that gap is where all the magic happens and the beauty of life is seen. In that gap is where all the peace, joy and freedom resides. But more importantly, as you rise beyond the mind, you will see the reality that you are the nonphysical and not the seemingly physical world itself. You will see that truth is not what you think or imagine it to be...but that it is right in front of you in this present moment. You will see you are one with this moment. This is what spirituality is – going beyond the limitations of the body-mind. It is about transcending a false mental identity that is trapped by its own thought-made prison walls and therefore is subject to the illusion of time and the misery of its own programming.

Practical Exercise: *Another powerful practice we can do at any time is to stand guard at the door of the mind and silently watch and wait for the next thought to appear.*

We can ask ourselves the question **'What thought will occur next?'**, *and quite simply we pause and view objectively, whatever thought comes into our mind next. See if you can watch it come and go. See if you can catch the thought with awareness.*

What you may discover is that objectively watching the mind does something interesting to the activity of mind. That is, that the mind appears to either be empty of thoughts...or that no thought lasts long under the gazing presence of awareness. All thoughts dissolve when they are being fully watched attentively. It's as if the very look and touch of awareness makes thoughts evaporate immediately. It's like...one minute you are being molested by the thoughts...and then as soon as you pay them conscious attention...they disappear in a puff of smoke! Therein lies the key: just consciously witness thoughts and they will start to be cleaned out one by one until only the pure undiluted consciousness remains.

This practice is especially good to do at times of heavy mind turbulence. Watching the mind in this way will allow it to slow down or even stop it dead in its tracks! And most of all, it instantaneously moves you to the position of the witness - which is always outside the circle of the thinking mind. The act of witnessing alone transports you beyond the dimension of time and thought, into the present reality.

Take a deep breath in. Stop and watch, without thought or discrimination. Create a break in the pattern of thinking. Do this for a couple of seconds at a time.

When we go ahead and look from our true position as the supreme witness, we may find ourselves becoming identified with the mind and falling back into it from time to time, just from shear habit. This is ok and is likely to happen, as long as we remind ourselves that 'Ah, I believed the mind' and then return to the experience of witnessing once again, all will be well.

What we may eventually discover is that the mind has

less and less of a pull on us and that we are able to consciously stay witnessing thoughts for longer and longer periods. As the supreme witness, we stay undisturbed and immoveable in what happens and whatever experiences arise. In silently witnessing inner and outer events we are completely free from their effects, as they can only touch the physical and not our nonphysical nature as the witnessing intelligence. Nothing can harm our eternal indestructible essence!

Here is a self-investigation question that we can ask ourselves at any time, especially if we once again find ourselves identified with thinking.

We ask the question: 'Who am I?'

When we ask this question, what we are really asking is two things: 'Who am I not?' and 'Who am I?'

As you have now discovered through your own observing and investigation, you are not the thinking mind and world of appearing forms and experiences.

So who then are you?

Well, there is no word that can describe that, no word or concept will do. But we can say **'I am the silent witness'**. Then to really answer the question in an experiential way, we **go to the experience of being**

the witness, to a position of the witnessing intelligence itself.

This is the difference between having an intellectual answer, which doesn't mean anything, compared to going to the actual experience of the silent witness. One is intellectual and the other is awakening itself.

So if one ever finds they are lost in the mind, they can ask this question as a reminder of what they are not, and as a means to move back to the throne of the supreme witness intelligence that they are.

Your true nature is free from the fluctuation of life's changing forms. You are prior to it all... you are the Infinite-Self... the Eternal Being.

You are that which is free from the flux of the world. You are resting in the immanence of reality. In this way, you are at the heart of experience whilst also not the experience itself. It's a divine paradox that can't be understood through thought... only through the direct experience of being.

As we rise above the level of the intellect, we begin to create a union between the physical and nonphysical dimensions. This bridging of the two happens in our immediate timeless experience. Our transcendence is the journey from the head into the heart... the heart of the universe which dwells in all beings. It is an instant shift from the darkness of ignorance (*unconsciousness*) into the light of truth (*consciousness*), and it happens as quickly as darkness leaves a room when the light switch is flicked on.

Practical Exercise: *Live from the heart*

Whatever challenging feelings, thoughts, situations or people come, meet and dissolve them all with the loving heart and embrace of pure presence.

Instead of struggling and resisting against these certain encounters, let them in and meet them with the open allowance of your loving witnessing presence, which is the love of god itself.

Encounter what comes not with judgement but with the acceptance of unconditional love. See that the nondual nature that you are includes everything, and excludes nothing. It does not pick and choose what experiences to have or what is good or bad, it approaches all experiences with equality, seeing everything as valid and as a part of the one play of existence. In this awakening everything is seen as another expression of itself and as another expression of you. All is felt as yourself in the experience of true Enlightenment. When you meet all challenging experiences with unconditional love, you will be amazed how they will become transmuted in your presence. It is like you are King Midas himself: everything you touch with this loving presence turns to gold. This is the alchemical ability one has when they stand in the pure beingness.

The moment an experience enters your presence, it will be touched by the essence of the divine if you accept it fully and totally.

Move in life like this and you will make flowers grow wherever you go...

Just stay as the witnessing presence and include everything that makes itself known within your current experience... without exception... and you will conquer all with the heart. Stand as pure silent awareness whilst also being aware of the particulars of this moment, which means *to notice all phenomena in the here and now.* This is what it means to be aware here now. Awakening is an inclusive experience. So this synergy of the witnessing presence, is like a beautiful merging and union because everything is included **in** it and **as** it. Your point of witnessing is not in the world, yet there is this sense of alive beingness in the body when the attention of the supreme witnessing is placed upon it. This creates a grounding spot of centeredness firmly within the body and heart, yet also beyond it. It is a complete paradox to the intellect.

It's the merging of the nonphysical and physical together, both of which are ultimately one. It is the same as the images playing on a TV screen being the same as the TV itself. Or like the painting on a canvas being one with the canvas itself. The world of experiential phenomenon is a transitory play happening within the field of the Infinite-Self, and when it is seen and accepted as such... ultimate freedom becomes known.

Practical Exercise: *Instead of indulging in thinking become aware of your natural sense of presence here... right now.*

That means to subtly notice and feel the energy-body without the application of thought. As you are aware of the energy *(vital force/beingness)* in the body, become aware that you are aware of it.

In other words, bring part awareness to the body and part awareness to awareness itself. Bring some awareness to the aliveness of the being whilst at the same time keeping and turning awareness towards itself.

So our approach is to become very much grounded in this **vibrant aliveness** whilst also being very watchful of whatever takes place. Watching the thought activity, emotions and sensations and the moving world but in a different kind of way. It is like there is an implosion that occurs, revealing the sense of one-ness.

You become free from the world, yet simultaneously very much in the world. Or, another way to say it would be, that the finite dream-self ends, and what is left is **everything** and **no-thing** in harmony. What is left is the Infinite-Self as **all that is** and **is not**. What remains is space and all appearances floating in this space - like temporary bubbles floating to the top of the ocean and popping once they hit the surface.

Being in this place of the **witnessing presence** has a completely different quality to it. When thoughts or emotions arise, there is no apartness from them: instead they are met with an eternal embrace that includes everything and excludes nothing. Everything is experienced intensely and fully, whilst as the same time these experiences never blemish you, for how can space be blemished or cut?

It is the **oneness** and **non-duality** of life that is cradled in the arms of itself *through* and *as us*, the Infinite-Self.

When the mirage of being a personal finite-self that is identified with the body-mind ends, what remains is what was always already there: EVERYTHING!

The separation and apartness of duality ends, and a nondual embrace becomes our direct perception of reality and self. Through the witnessing presence, nothing is excluded and all of life flows into our divine spaciousness as if we are a mirror reflecting the phenomenal world back to itself. Everything is met instantaneously with this natural embrace, and instead of detaching from what appears... we instead go into it: entering **fully** into the experience of it.

The big difference is that we now enter the experience without losing ourselves in the experience, which occurred previously when we were mind identified as the finite-self. All experiences of thought, feelings and situations are met by the warm inclusiveness of our heart and openness, and in this way everything is transformed and transmuted into the pure source of the Infinite being. It is a center point that in essence, has no center. It is a pure paradox of the Infinite one existence that we are. In other words, when we discover ourselves as the witnessing intelligence and we place that intelligence upon any external object such as the body or anything outside the body, a merging happens: where the object becomes absorbed by our silent witnessing. A pure oneness is forever established and liberation becomes our direct experience.

Before, through the finite-self, we were keeping everything away from us, but now that the illusion has dropped away, everything is immediately available to us... **as us**. This is the total inclusiveness of our true enlightened nature.

Section 3
Relationships And Communication For Self-Realization

11 - Daily Interactions to Deepen in Awakening

True connection can only happen when you show up totally.

Our daily lives are often filled with interactions of many kinds. Whether with friends and family, at work or in the street, all of these meetings and interactions can be used as a way to reconfirm who we really are.

In fact, all experiences can be used in this way. In the midst of all experiences lies the one that is aware of the experience. Without this awareness of an experience there could be no experience of any kind, and so each experience can be a reference to turn back towards our essential nature at any time and to recognize who we are in that present experience. This is the same with all relationships and communication of any kind. All things can point us back home to the Infinite beingness. Also, as all events we encounter are always only happening in the present, and the present is where we reside, each experience if given our full attention can lead us back to the now reality in which it is occurring.

Many people often speak of the difficulty of losing themselves in the everyday affairs they engage in. But in reality, you can never be lost, because if you were really lost when associating with others you would not know about it. You would not be able to report on such a thing, because what was it that was able to be aware of a sense of being *'lost'*? In other words, without the awareness of the situation and experience there could be no experience!

So know that when you are with others and are engaged in any situation, that the **awareness** of which you really are is always present despite whether you think it is or not. All one has to do is notice it. Use the so called outer experience as a way to notice the one inside that is aware of it. The beauty of Self-Realization is that everything can become a confirmation of your *'aware beingness'* in the here now moment.

The basic and crucial element of all relationships and communication is the quality and wakefulness of one's *'witnessing presence'*. Without it, all interactions lose potency and aliveness, and all encounters become dull and unconscious in value.

All that life is ever asking of you is to show up fully and be aware here now. When you do this, you begin to experience a richness of life that you have never tasted before. You imbue all life situations with a quality of energy that allows the sun to shine wherever you go. People will feel your potent presence at all times in all situations.

Life can be truly magical and comes alive through the natural enhanced perception of pure awareness.

12 - Amorous Relationships

Don't seek to control… instead accept and enjoy.
Our whole society has been brought up on the idea that a romantic relationship is the missing piece to ones sense of completeness and happiness. We say things like *'he or she completes me'* or *'without them I'm nothing'*. This is a grave misperception that the conditioned self holds, and which places our happiness and fulfillment at the mercy of another. The consequences of this untruth can cause a lot of suffering and unhappiness for us and those around us.

When we believe our happiness depends upon another, we will automatically seek to control the other in some way to get what we want, because we believe that if we don't get what we want from them we will be unhappy. In other words, we feel we must control them because our happiness depends upon it! This creates the controlling aspect of all relationships that we have seen or been a part of. A relationship like this will ultimately lead to misery and destruction. There is no freedom in that kind of relationship, only bondage.

Instead, a relationship where two people come together from a sense of **inner completeness** is a beautiful relationship that will blossom and flourish. This type of relationship will give each person in the relationship a chance to enjoy being with each other, rather than trying to control one another in order to gain something from them.

When we don't try to seek our sense of fulfillment or happiness from another, rather accept ourselves and the other as true and complete, we let go of the *'need'* to control the relationship. When we are not focused on controlling the relationship, but simply being present with another, we are in a space to enjoy and appreciate the other person far greater, from a place of purity and unconditional love.

The truth is, there is no person or thing that can complete you. That is because you are already complete. You were born a complete package with your eternal essence already in place. All one has to do is uncover that through present moment recognition, then one will discover and feel their inherent sense of completeness instantly. Don't believe any thought that would try to tell you otherwise, because any thoughts are just the running programs of the conditioned mind. We have often been taught that we must do, be or obtain something more to be fulfilled - which is a lie. What you seek is already where you are. You are right where you are, and the inherent sense of fulfillment automatically comes with the presence of your being. What you are cannot come or go, and therefore nothing can be taken nor can it be given. You are the Eternal Being.

Be aware of how the mind seeks a partner in the belief that you will be complete if you acquire one. Watch the conditioned minds tendency to seek a partner. Notice that belief and question its validity: **is it really true that you need a partner to be complete?**

As you notice this thought/belief, become aware of your natural sense of completeness within. Feel the alive-aware internal presence that you are.

The seeking of control doesn't just happen in romantic relationships, it can also happen in many other kinds of interactions too. The finite-identity at its core lives in a state of fear. This is because it believes and feels itself to be separate from the rest of existence. Because of this it will seek to control as many things as possible for fear of not getting what it wants, therefore feeling unpleasant or unhappy. The finite-identity is in the ultimate state of lack. Lack meaning - to perceive itself as being alone and isolated from everything, and so it seeks to find its fulfillment and connection from the outside, from people, circumstance and possessions.

It will hold onto as many things as possible in order to plump its identity up, because ultimately... it seeks to become Infinite and Eternal. It wishes to live forever... It wishes to live forever because it fears death... or more specifically... the loss or death of identity which is its biggest fear. So with that, a partner is one way it often falsely believes it can cling and hold on to life, or so it believes.

This means that it will always use people and situations

as a means to an end, or quite simply, to get what it wants. This can take form in the subtlest of ways - from trying to win an argument, trying to get your own way, or trying to get someone to do what you want them to do or to be. The finite-self is always looking to manipulate the world for its own gain. But the 'gain' is actually an illusion that slips through one's fingers like sand. It will never last or add anything to it, and then when it disappears, it will always feel a sense of lack again. This is the cruel game the conditioned-mind plays with itself with our consent - and by consenting we become hostage to its game. This game can last lifetimes... and for most beings it does, until we eventually wake up: which can only be done in the now.

The only way to end that game is to discover that which can never be given or taken away from you. To discover the **everlasting immortal self**, the Infinite being that you inherently are. The one that resides in this moment.

Practical Exercise: *If you, or someone you know is in a romantic relationship take the time to reflect and notice how the finite-mind-identity seeks to control the other in order to get what it wants so that it can feel good and satisfied.*

See how the conditioned-self has an attachment to the other person for its own satisfaction. As a practice – consciously **let go** of trying to control relationships. See if you can just **allow** them to be as they are and **accept** them totally. See if you can **enjoy** the relationship as it is, by being present and showing up fully with the totality of your being.

Another way in which the conditioned-self seeks to control relationships, is through its expectations of the other person and expectations of the relationship itself.

Often at times through the finite-identity, we may have certain ideas in mind about what we want, how things should be, what the other person should be giving us or where the relationship should be heading. These are all ideas which have been picked up from society through social conditioning and our up-bringing. The conditioned-identity has it all mapped out in its head, all strategically planned so that it can achieve what it believes is going to make it fulfilled and happy.

When we allow the conditioned-self to take over in this way, we dishonor reality in two ways. First, is that we can never fully appreciate the present because we are seeking to be somewhere in the future *(a future that will never come)*. Second, we end up using our partner as a means to get what we want. So rather than truly being with them, we may end up subtly using them instead. This is not true love but is instead a conditional type of 'love': a 'love' that requires and expresses itself in - 'I must get what I want otherwise I no longer love you'.

The nature of the Infinite-Self however, is not like this. It naturally and spontaneously allows all things to be as they are in this moment - and from this place of inherent allowance, things begin to flow more smoothly. It has the willingness to meet whatever comes with openness and ease. It allows people and situations to be as they are instead of struggling against them. The Infinite-Self is already complete and is not looking to complete itself by holding another hostage to its demands.

Practical Exercise: *Let go of the need to fulfill future relationship expectations. Instead just savior and enjoy the relationship now in the present.*

You can't be here if you are in the future, and you can't enjoy **now** if you are focused on being somewhere else. Learn to be present and appreciate the relationship in the here and now. Relax and go deeper into the experience of being with your partner in the present. Often times we are so focused on things leading somewhere else or becoming 'better' that we don't give the being (partner) in front of us our full attention now. Therefore we lose the depth of our connection with another. We often overlook them for an image or ideal that we have created in the mind, and when we are in mind… we are not being present.

We have all been given a false model of love that states: if I give you something then you must give me something in return. It's like a business deal: a superficial transaction based on selfish motives. Which is also, essentially what marriage is: a contract of vows that *"must"* or *"should"* be contractually fulfilled.

Another area of influence which conditions our thoughts and ideas of relationships, is religion and subsequent *'ideals'*. This type of **'contract relationship'** that many of us may have experienced is not true unconditional love. It's a love that is based on conditions. A love that can quickly turn to disdain or hate if the conditions we have set are no longer being met. Unconditional love on the other hand, means to love without any conditions. It's a boundless love that has no expectations on how and when love should be there, or in what way it *"should"* be expressed. It's a love that spring from a place of purity. You love the other for who they are, as they are, and not what you are seeking to gain from them. By loving them for who they are you give them freedom: freedom and space to be themselves. This is true unconditional love.

When we live from **present-open-awareness** and drop the programmed mind, unconditional love becomes a natural by-product. We find ourselves being more presently available with our partner and being more accepting of who they are **now** and of the relationship **as it is** currently. From here something even more beautiful may begin to occur. We may find that we start to connect more deeply with our partner on a level that we may have never experienced previously before. And because of that a greater intimacy is born. This deeper level of intimacy arises because we start to see the enormous depth of being in the other, rather than the surface or superficial layer we were so focused on once before. Shifting to this space of **unconditional-acceptance** we start to enjoy the relationship immensely, each moment at a time. The relationship becomes a true adventure of discovery and enjoyment rather than a struggling game of control and dissatisfaction. As a consequence of our true love we become more relaxed: we open our hearts and ourselves, and by doing so naturally move more with the flow, excited to experience and explore the moment together.

Practice: Display unconditional love in relationships. Unconditional love means total acceptance and allowance of that person. See if you can accept your partner just the way they are - without trying or wanting them to change or be different.

When you act from a space of unconditional love and acceptance, one of the amazing things that can happen is that you and your partner begin to harmonize with each other. You become more accepting, appreciative and grateful for who they are. This does not mean you cannot speak up if something doesn't feel right, but what it does mean is that it enhances your communication, connection and understanding. You first **accept** what it is they have done, said or how they are *(you accept what is occurring in the present reality)*, and then from a place of *non-opposition, non-judgment* and acceptance you can then respond in a calm, clear and conscious way. We respond best when we see clearly, and we can only see clearly when we are not blinded by the judgements and resistance of the mind. Instead of being in opposition to this moment, we align with it. In doing so, we gain greater energy and clarity to deal with whatever is presented before us in the moment.

In this way what you say will be communicated with a tremendous power and authority, rather than coming from a place of being overwhelmed with emotion or anger, because when you react in the latter way it only tends to put the other person on the defensive. There is nothing more powerful than someone who can speak their truth from a place of inner completeness, calm and centeredness. When you are natural with others, and remain your authentic self, you will draw them into the state of being more natural themselves - and a true heart to heart connection will be formed.

13 - Everyday Interactions

The quality of our interactions depends upon the quality of existence we embody.

Unless you live in a cave, it's likely you encounter people on a daily basis. These could be friends, family, work colleagues or meeting new people for the first time. The way in which we interact with each being says a lot about whether we are awake or whether we are sleep-walking through life. The conditioned-self lives through the past, and so it sees people through the lens of yesterday's information and experiences. This means that the conditioned-self is not capable of meeting the **now moment** in a true way and therefore it never meets people in a true way either. Nothing is ever new or fresh for the conditioned-self... as it is always polluting this moment and the people in it by dragging past thinking into the present. It never really sees what is here because it is only viewing what is here through past projections.

Through the identity of the false-self we develop a type of unconscious unwritten agreement, and that is: ***I'll pretend you are who you 'think' you are if you pretend I am who I 'think' I am.*** And so, via the filter of collective-thought we tend to always see each other through a past overlay, an overlay of past information and experiences. We often react to people we know in the same old predictable ways, seeing them in the same way through our memory of them. It can become very robotic: as in, this person says this type of thing…and I react in this way or by saying this… same old same old. These are the karmic patterns that keeps us locked into the past and leave us destined to repeat it. We become trapped in a kind of perpetual '*Groundhog Day*'.

The way in which we ultimately change and become free from all karma…is by letting go of all past thought and identity with it, and by returning our awareness to the reality of this **eternal moment:** full of vibrant life and Infinite possibilities. There is no karma for the **eternal-self,** which means that the past as memory no longer burdens us. We suddenly see freshly and therefore can act freshly and interact in brand new ways. Ways which are not rigid, predictable or fixed by belief systems of the past - but are flexible and relevant to the situation before us. Our true nature is adaptable, and it changes with whatever the situation requires. We are like a transparent mirror that reflects what is required in the present, and the response always happens spontaneously - never cunningly.

Practical Exercise: *Meet people as if for the first time with fresh eyes.*

Instead of seeing people and holding them hostage to past preconceptions, relax all past thoughts about them and see them with the clear sight of the present tense. Be willing to experience people freshly in the now moment and to interact with them from pure awareness, rather than any conditioned past thoughts.

See them **as they are** and not as the conditioned-self *'thinks'* they are. Don't judge them, be nondiscriminatory in your approach. You will find yourself directly experiencing them in a whole new way, then you can meet freshly together.

Nondiscrimination and the State of knowing that we do not Know

Judging a person does not define who they are, it defines who you are, because you are the one holding it.

The way in which we think and make judgements in life is simply a reflection of what opinions we ourselves are holding at that moment. It is almost like holding-up a mirror to our psyche, and when we judge a situation we are not seeing *'what is'* but only our mental definition of *'what is'* which is not necessarily correct and can never be ultimately true. This subjective judgement therefore is telling us more about where we are at and what we are holding onto ourselves as opposed to who or what the situation is.

*Our judging or non-judgement reveals to us where our perception is and whether or not we are aligned with the **truth...** which is the **'Is-ness'** of the moment, reality*

as it is *itself.*

Sometimes the things we initially label as *'bad'* turn out to be the most wonderful things possible...and sometimes not. Life ebbs and flows and all we know for sure is that one thing always flows into the next. In other words, stop trying to understand and let life just be life. Let ***'what is, be what is'*** without trying to understand or define it. When we relax the need to judge or understand a great freedom will arise, and we can find ourselves in the wisdom of the Is-ness of existence without any explanation. Lost in the beauty of the universe in its most pure form.

Life can be full of contradictions. Without deconstruction there is no opportunity for trans-formation and without the bust there is no boom. Without racism in America there would have been no rise of the great Martin Luther King to oppose it and inspire and shed light on issues that may have never come to the surface without him. Without hot there could be no cold; each one depends on the other in a sense, and so it is impossible to say what is good or bad or whether anything is ultimately positive or negative in this reality, as both depend on each other for their existence. All can be used as a guiding light to uncover awareness and recognize our innate freedom.

Both the so called *'good'* and *'bad'* merge into one, from where no distinctions can be made. It is like a paint brush stroke on the wall going from thick paint to a lighter and lighter shade... until the paint runs out and can no longer be seen. Where in that line of paint can you pin-point the exact moment it goes from dense to light? In between dense and light there are an Infinite amount of shades. In between dark and light or good and bad there are also Infinite shades, and each one merges into the other, all creating the single **one** stroke of existence.

Without one of the shades... there would be a break in the chain, meaning it no longer could or would be one. All is an expression of the Infinite, and the Infinite has no inherent meaning built into it. Only the programmed mind (what has been learnt) prescribes meanings to things where there are none. Realizing this is truly liberating, as it frees you from the bounds of a dual reality existing only in the mind.

When we venture beyond the idea of good and bad, beyond the appearance of duality, we arrive at the place of truth which neutralizes and harmonizes both. All becomes accepted as equal and valid, all just different aspects of the same one existence.

We often waste so much time and energy on judging people, situations and circumstances through our societal conditioning. It is often negative judgements and definitions that are brought to bear, and these negative judgements if believed only serve to bring our state of energy down, as our beliefs can easily translate into inner struggle and therefore unpleasant emotions within us. Our judgements create our suffering and can be an influencing factor to make others suffer around us.

As many past sages and philosophers have spoken about, one of the greatest realizations that can happen in our lives is that we come to a place where everything we think about ourselves and the world comes into question. A place that puts into question all the things that we believed to be true about ourselves and the world. It is where we suddenly realize that through the guise of the mind and thought... that we cannot know a single thing to be true for sure. It's an understanding that the mind is not the tool for the job when it comes to making contact with reality. To come to this realization, we must first admit that we don't really know the truth. It is only then that our exploration can truly begin.

Realizing we do not know takes us from being a believer into a seeker. One can only reach truth when one becomes a seeker first, because a believer already believes they know and therefore will not search for the real truth. A belief becomes a block and makes one more ignorant of life (not knowing life) because it takes them further away from reality and keeps them lost in the head. It puts up a barrier so that one cannot meet reality face to face. Only through direct experience of life in the present can we know the truth of existence and our own being, of which both are one and the same. This is the beginning of real knowing: what real know-ledge is.

This is the difference between belief and direct knowing. Belief is always secondhand information that you have picked up from someone or somewhere, and then stored it in the mind to carry with you everywhere you go. Direct knowing however is vastly differently. Direct knowing comes from the being-level of who we are. It is a firsthand knowing that is acquired when we explore the present moment directly.

The only thing that we can truly know is our direct experience in this moment, and it's in this moment that we find life's true reality. Truth is not conceptual, it cannot be a belief, because a belief is always about something that is outside our present moment experience. Truth is experiential, and it is realized through our direct experience of it in the now reality.

When we realize that no thought or concept is true, nor ever can be, and that we actually don't know what anything really is, then we move into the innocence of **'knowing that we do not know'**: our true home beyond the mind and finite-self. Knowing that we do not know is different than *'not knowing'*, because when we **know** we do not know, then we have taken a step towards true conscious awareness…maybe for the first time. Whereas just *'not knowing'* is simply a mind identities ignorance of truth. There is no degree of conscious awareness there, it's a very different state.

This is the starting point of all real wisdom and truth, because only from this place of *'knowing we don't know'* will we be open to seeing the true reality that lay before us. In this realization we are not clouded or blinded by anything.

So in regards to our daily interactions with people, the same truth applies - Stop judging people or attaching labels to them. Stop holding preconceived notions, ideas, expectations or falsities against people. Rather allow and let people be people. We all have the ability to meet others from a space that has no name. To meet them from the place of inner quietness at the core of our being, beyond the personal discriminations of the mind. And when we operate from a place which is absent of judgement, we set ourselves and others free. Life is but a slightly delayed mirror of the mind. What we think and believe often begins to echo in what we call the external world. If you only display your pure free nature beyond thought, then life reflects that back in each moment. Suddenly you see reality instead of a distortion.

Practical Exercise: *Notice how the conditioned-self easily throws up thoughts of judgements about people, and how it labels them or creates a story around them. For instance* **'I don't like this person'**, *or* **'What they have done is wrong'**. *Notice how the conditioned-self is always looking to create mental distinctions that only serves to create a barrier between you and another.*

Instead of believing and indulging in the judgmental thoughts, refrain by seeing that it is not you that is casting the judgement, but it is instead the habit of the programmed mind. Instead, stay present and go to the actual inner experience of the **disengaged witness** of the thoughts.

Be as the **silent witness** and watch the **thinker** as it seeks to judge and define people. Remember, no thought is ultimately true, only seeing reality *'as it is'* is true. See them as they are - not as the mind says they are. I assure you, that when you do this, you will experience an enormous freedom. It will feel like an elephant being taken off of your shoulders. You will start to feel a great peace come over you, because when we believe the judgements in our head...it only causes us to feel unwell inside, and it only creates resistance and therefore an unpleasant feeling or emotion within us. If we view or judge someone as *'bad'*, then we feel bad and unpleasant inside. Un-pleasant emotions arise because of our judgement, and these discriminations only serve to blind us to the true reality that is before us.

If we are able to catch the judgement before we believe it, then that is very powerful. If however, we find ourselves sparked with a certain emotion on behalf of already believing a judgement, we can do this practice:

Practical Exercise: *Take a quiet pause after anger, stress, fear and doubt or any emotion that may arise.*

When we feel a certain emotion in response to something that we are thinking or believing about the outside world or about a person, we can take a short quiet pause of **inner stillness**. This gives us a space of non-reaction to the emotion. In this **quiet pause** there is a space of freedom from the emotion and there is a moment of consciousness. We allow ourselves to be with it, but the pause means we don't mentally stir it any further with more thoughts about the emotion. On our part there is a willingness to allow the emotion in without resistance to it, and in this way, it dissolves in our presence.

When we believe a thought an emotion arises with it, and when the emotion comes...more thoughts come to feed the emotion. The emotion then becomes stronger, and before we know it we have whipped up a mind/body frenzy of emotion that seems to consume us. This emotion blinds us from the truth, and that goes for all emotions. Even being overly excited about something can cloud our perception about what we are seeing. When we awaken, all good qualities are there inherently, and we would not sacrifice that for any overwhelming emotion.

The quiet pause practice breaks that mind-body chain and allows us to neutralize its cycle.

It is like stepping off of a hamster wheel of thoughts and emotions so that we can break free from its cycle and reset ourselves from a place of **pure witnessing**. So anytime a strong emotion makes itself known, just take a short quiet pause and see what happens.

It is an especially powerful practice to do if we find ourselves in an argument with someone or if we are having stressful thoughts about a person. This practice helps us find the inner solace and calm in the storm, it allows us to find the space in the clutter and the stillness in the turbulence. If one goes into the quiet pause totally... then all emotions eventually dissolve and the body resets itself in the view of our **aware awake presence**.

14 - Conscious Communication

Communal wellbeing is central to human life.

Just as cells in a body must communicate with each other to function, so must human beings. Real communication is the absolute foundation of human existence, but so often miscommunication or the lack of communication altogether occurs.

Conscious communication only occurs when we are fully alert and awake in the present moment. If we allow ourselves through mental processes to aimlessly wander into the past and future, then it becomes impossible to communicate properly and consciously with others, because that would mean we are not fully **'here'** with them. Conscious communication is all about intimacy and connection to the being with whom we are attempting to communicate. To **'commune'** literally means to **'be with'** and to *'be with'* someone means that we need to communicate effectively at all times.

To be fully aware and ready for communication means being one hundred percent present in the moment and giving our full attention and awareness to another being. True communication happens heart to heart, when we see the **beingness** of another, not the *'person'*, then we have a real heart connection. The **person** is a mental collection from the past, a personality made up of thoughts and conditioning. The beingness is the true deeper essence of who we are communicating with in the present - the same essence that we ourselves are.

So the bedrock of all conscious communication is a great state of **'hereness'**, which is to say, to be in the moment with another fully and totally from your heart.

To **be** with them means to **'being'** with them, or in other words, your beingness with their beingness, a true heart to heart connection.

All that is needed for this to occur, is to show up for them fully: without carrying a past or future with you.

Practical Exercise: *Very simply practice being more present with people. Give them your full undivided attention, and see what happens.*

You may discover that people warm to you and are more likely to share themselves with you. A bond will be created, one heart speaking to another. As it is often very rare that a being fully shows up with another, they will feel a huge difference being in your presence, whether they are consciously aware of it or not. If you are fully present with another, then even to share silence with them will still make them feel at home in your presence. Such is the power and potency of your inner core essence.

Each time you commune with another in this way, you are deepening in your own state of natural beingness, becoming ever more conscious and awake. When it all comes down to it, at the ultimate level of existence, all communication is the **'one'** existence experiencing and communicating back to itself.

This is the true secret of non-dual existence: all beings are just another you in disguise. When you turn your full undiluted awareness towards another, without thought in it, a merging will take place and in that moment...you both consciously become one. This is true intimacy and true communion.

15 - Conscious Listening

The biggest communication problem is that we do not listen to understand...we listen to reply.

Have you ever been speaking with someone but get the sense that they are not really listening to you?

That maybe they are lost in thinking about something else or that they are just waiting for their turn to speak without really listening to what you have to say?

When this happens, the other person is not really listening to what you have to say but are instead waiting to counteract your words with their own thoughts and this in effect means that they do not really hear what you are saying, but are only hearing their own mind's interpretations of your words. It is impossible to focus our full attention on listening when part of our attention is concentrating on how to respond and part of it is busy lost in thinking.

So true listening is about **receptivity**, which means how receptive we are to what is being given to us. If we are busy thinking and are not fully in the moment with another, then how can we truly be receptive to what is given? If we are unreceptive because we are not really *'here'*, then anything being received will be blocked-out by our mind.

Real listening occurs when we are empty of thought in that moment. If we are full of thoughts then there is no room for the speech that is being given to us by another. How can you fully listen to their broadcast if your own radio channel is playing over the top of it?

If you are **full** you will miss, if you are empty you will receive fully.

Practical Exercise: *When listening to another speak, see if you can remain quiet and empty inside, maybe by bringing your attention down from your mind into your heart level in the chest and focus on their words and the sound of the words as opposed to mentally trying to interpret them.*

Allow the words to be received naturally, and allow yourself to feel the words instead of mentally pro-cessing them in your mind.

What we may notice with this practice is just how often the mind tries to 'grab' the words and make sense of them and how it wants to automatically respond immediately. At first this practice may feel quite strange, but the more we **'feel'** the words and feel the other persons being, the result will be pleasantly surprising and the other person will also feel more deeply connected to us.

This practice is excellent in developing the capacity to become more calm and quiet within. It gets us in touch with the *'being'* level of who we essentially are. The more intently we listen, the more meditative and *'silent'* we become. The more meditative and silent we become...the more peaceful and joyful we become also. This then forms the basis for a powerful depth of presence to flower within us.

16 - Conscious Speech

Watch what you say, because words are your spells. They either spin the web of illusion or reinforce your alignment with reality.

Conscious speech occurs when we allow it to emanate from deep within the *'quiet place'* inside of us. This helps bypass the conditioned state of consciousness and transports us into a place of **pure being**.

One of the simplest ways to enter this *'quiet place'* is to get more in touch with the body by placing our attention upon it.

When we are grounded and feel our bodies totally, we divert attention away from the busyness of the thinking mind and instead move it more into the body itself, thus reducing the mind's activity and opening-up a space of greater silence and stillness within and from whence a more intense state of intelligence and expression can be found.

In this way our words become more intuitive and spontaneous as they spring forth from silence and not from the past information being held in the forefront of the mind.

The second step of conscious speech is to be fully aware of the words we are speaking and to choose those words very carefully, instead of just unconsciously saying the first thing that occurs to us from the forefront of thoughts spiraling around in the mind.

Unconscious speech in action means that we are not totally aware of what we are doing, and so in this case we are speaking without really noticing what is being said. Below is a simple practice to undertake before speaking.

Practical Exercise: *Firstly, we need to make sure that we undergo the listening practice when hearing another speak. Then rather than speaking ourselves immediately after they have spoken, take a deep breath and a short, silent pause before choosing the most brief and precise words with which to reply.*

In other words, you make contact with the innermost place of quietness at the core of your being, and from there we can speak in a more clear and precise manner without using an unnecessary amount of words.

Often many people speak unconsciously and therefore waste energy because they are not being attentive of their speech and the words they are using. When we practice the exercise above, we should find ourselves becoming more conscious and will no longer be wasting energy in using many unnecessary words.

Every time we speak unconsciously from the conditioned state, we create and reinforce more layers of illusion. Our experience then supports these illusions.

However, the more we express intuitively from inner silence, the greater our experience of a true harmonized reality becomes. Our speech can either pull us further into the web of illusion or it can get our mind onboard with seeing reality clearly in order to support our awakening.

If you find yourself not able to be present with the people you communicate with, then let that be a good reminder to use these opportunities as a way to practice presence.

Use the time you spend with people as a way to deepen in your spiritual practice. Allow each interaction to be a way to notice the present moment and live from that space of open free aware presence.

Be like a lighthouse that people flock to, just so they can seek solace around you and be able tune into the same quiet presence you exude.

Being empty and present is like the purest form of meditation possible, and so the more you practice this... the more you will be in your meditation, then others will fall into meditation with you also.

Section 4
The Joy Of Being In Action

The Joy of Being in Action

The discovery of your life force is a truly fulfilling and satisfying experience. This experience is the joy of being, and we take this with us wherever we go.

It is all very well being conscious and feeling our aliveness in the privacy of our own homes, but how can we bring this greater awareness of who we really are into our everyday actions and activities?

How can we infuse action with a supreme quality of consciousness of the likes we have never been operating from before?

Many times, without knowing, people unconsciously suffer and perform worse in the everyday actions that they undertake because of this unconsciousness. Whether it be at work or even in a sport or leisure activity, most beings split themselves in two. A part of them is here **now** in this moment, while the other part of them is in the **future** anticipating some future result, attainment or escape. Or, they are here now while their attention is lost in the memories of the past.

This split of the body and mind creates an inner turmoil and imbalance that most beings hardly recognize anymore because it has become the normal way of life for most. Our whole society is based in past and future so much that it creates an inner division in the minds and hearts of men, and so the quality of people's actions are reduced and the joy in which actions are meant to be done from greatly diminishes.

The real secret to a greater awareness and joy in action, is to see the difference between a human being and a human doing...

17 - Human Being vs Human Doing

Wherever you go you cannot escape yourself. Your 'being' is primary and 'doing' is always secondary. To put the latter first... is to put the cart before the horse.

What we must come to realize is that we are firstly **'human beings'** not **'human doings'**. **Doing** implies a separate entity that thinks it is *'someone'* doing *'something'* to get *'something'* so that it can get *'somewhere'*. That's the prime illusion spoke of earlier.

*'If you think you are a **someone**... going **somewhere**... to try and get **something**... that is going to amount to **something**, suffering will occur, because this prime illusion is what makes most people operate in a false sense of time and separateness'.*

A human doing is always living in a perception of time and operating mostly in an unconscious state. They have very little quality of **hereness** in what they are engaged in because they have their attention in the morrow and not in the present.

They are so focused on an image in their mind that they never become attentively conscious of this moment and the action they are undertaking in it. A **human doing** is blind to the moment because they only see the moment as something to look past to get to something else. They see it as a hurdle to cross, and they are never fully present and therefore are not totally alive or aware.

So the real key to all conscious action is *'being'*: to *'be'* before to *'do'*. In other words, don't **do** actions to get to some imaginary place or result in your head. Instead, *just be the action itself*, which means that we are fully present in each action that we take. In that sense we become the action in and of itself.

Practical Exercise: *As you next take action, instead of getting lost in thinking about what you are doing, bring some of your attention to the sense of being. Feel your natural beingness in the present underneath the action, and then proceed with the action you are taking.*

What you will notice is that you feel more grounded, centered and happy when taking action, as opposed to being largely in your head. The quality of your action will increase because you will be able to pay full attention to it and not get distracted by mental chatter and imagery.

I remember I was once hitting some boxing pads when I was younger, and I was hitting them very accurately while I was paying full attention, then I got distracted by a future thought and I ended up missing one of the pads completely. This is what the mind often does to people all the time. It takes you away from now and keeps you in the head. By living in the mind... you miss reality. It's, only by stepping out of the mind that you can come into true contact with reality.

As you are able to be more present in the midst of all actions, you will perform better at what you do and will feel much happier. To be present in action is a tremendously fulfilling experience, and so because of this natural fulfillment, every action will become a pure joy for you.

18 - Breaking out of Mechanical Actions

Unconscious action is a dead action, robotic. But action with full awareness breathes life into all that you do.

The conditioned self is constantly in autopilot mode. It knows no other way, and it is inherent in its pro-gramming to act in unconscious and mechanical ways. It moves in a very predictable manner.

Conscious action means to break out of dead mech-anical movements and to bring a new aliveness to that which we do. Conscious action is **alive** action!

When we act through the conditioned mind, we operate in an unaware way in which we don't pay full attention to what it is that is being done. For instance, have you ever been driving in your car and have had to remind yourself to pay attention because you were off in your head day-dreaming about something?

For the majority of people, it is a regular occurrence that happens most of the time, in many situations throughout the day. One minute they are paying attention, conscious of what they are doing, the next moment drifting into unconsciousness, day-dreaming or thinking about something completely unrelated to the task at hand.

It's like brushing your teeth in the morning. You have done it so many times that you give it very little attention. All you want to do is get it over and done with, so you can be somewhere else. The conditioned-self makes many things like this a stepping stone to get past and overlook. Because of this habit one misses out on their own **joy of being** in the moment. Before you know it... your whole life has passed by in unconsciousness, and you then find yourself one day having a moment of consciousness... asking... where did my whole life go?

When we are unconsciousness our whole life can seem like a blur, but with consciousness our experience of life becomes crystal clear. The ones that are un-conscious miss the centeredness that comes when you give each action, no matter how small, your full undivided attention. Which really means that you give yourself your full attention, because you can only be **here**... and nowhere else. So it's no wonder one feels ungrounded and mistakes are made when they are not here. How can one display a true and deep quality of being if they are not fully present?

Practical Exercise: *Just pay attention!*

See if you can catch yourself when you next find you are performing an unconscious automatic action, and instead... do the action with your full conscious attention. Just be fully present and aware whilst per-forming the action. **Feel** the **sense** of the action as you do it. This simply means: *be in your body not in your head and experience the action directly through a position and quality of presence.*

This could be as simple as moving your body, making a cup of tea or washing the dishes. Pay more attention to what you do and bear witness to a different quality and grace of movement beyond the normal un-consciousness of action. By moving in a conscious way, you will breathe new life into all of your movements and they will take on a new quality and meaning, and in doing so you will move more joyously in everything that you do.

19 - Authentic Joy and Non Attachment

Joy cannot exist when attachment is present, because only more fear can come from attachment. Drop attachment and you will drop fear, then authentic joy blossoms naturally.

The conditioned-self clings to objects to be happy, not realizing that the clinging itself is also the source of its unhappiness. They are too sides of the same coin, the thing that can make you happy one moment can also make you unhappy the next. This is because you have become dependent on it. Anything that belongs to the phenomenal world has the potential to be changed or taken away, and so if you try to rely upon those things for happiness you will always experience unhappiness with it.

One of the first things we are taught as we grow and develop, is that in order to be joyful or fulfilled in this world, we must be successful. The western interpretation of success is basically the acquiring of material possessions, status, admiration and achievements. We are basically taught that the determination of our joy comes through the right external circumstances being in place.

Society says joy is *'that which pleases us from our external situations'*, but what is actually being suggested here is that real joy is **reasonless**.

Real joy is *'that which is naturally present within us when we are not blocking or hindering it through mental attachments created by societal programs. It is our natural state of being - Internal causeless joy.'*

The first is a feeling that appears to be triggered by the outside; the second is an internal state of being that comes naturally when one is just being their **original self** in the **present** without needing or attaching to anything in particular. One is caused and one is causeless. One is inherent and one is acquired.

Causeless joy is the perfume that emits from our natural state of being when we are being **aware** in the now moment, just the same way that a beautiful flower emits its scent. It occurs when we are not in a relentless pursuit of happiness from the external world and when we stop looking for something about which to be joyful for, then suddenly, joy will happen naturally and spontaneously. It will naturally appear within us, all because the absence of restlessness, is peace and joy.

Most of us, on a day-by-day basis are constantly looking to the *outside world* in our search for happiness: the next achievement, activity, compliment or relationship.

But if we could just end this relentless pursuit for a few moments, and allow everything to be **just as it is** with total acceptance, without trying to change or add anything, then what would be revealed to us is a pure natural state of inner joy; a joy that cannot be contained, an **ecstatic joy** wanting to burst to the surface, a state that is revealed as we relax more and more into ourselves in the here and now moment. Through identification of the mind one can often become enmeshed and mentally invested in many things for ones sense of fulfillment and joy. Here is a practice we can do as a reminder not to identify and therefore not become entangled in what externally does or does not occur.

Practical Exercise: *The next time a situation arises that is challenging or is not going the way you would prefer it to, say* **'I am not this situation, and I am not the outcome of this situation.'**

As you repeat the above mantra, you may suddenly feel more relaxed and notice a change in your level of awareness. Whatever arises, just allow it to be there.

Continue to remind yourself of this in each and every situation until it becomes completely natural for you to be aware of it, and you will begin to feel a great inner freedom arising within you.

Just as a dam stops water rushing into the river, so does seeking joy from the outside stop it from appearing naturally within us. It is the restless seeking and clinging of mind that obscures our inherent joy from naturally and spontaneously bubbling to the surface. When we look to the outside for happiness we overlook what is already present, and we miss who we are in this moment.

Practical Exercise: *Observe how the conditioned-self waits for permission from future outside situations to be joyful. Notice how it is always seeking joy in external objects.*

*Instead, drop these ideas and give yourself permission to experience **'the joy of being'** right here… right now.*
Let go of the mental clinging that happens on behalf of outside circumstances… by seeing that you are in-herently already enough and that the present (which you are one with) is complete in and of itself. See that you are already whole and that by your very existence you are fulfilled already. That nothing else can add anything more to the core of who you really are which is beyond circumstance and that which changes.

*No object, person, place or circumstance can give you who you really are, because who you are is already the case. It has always been this way and will always be so. Take a fresh look now and discover **who you are** and **what is here** in this moment.*

20 - Falling in Love with the Act not the Result

When you start to enjoy yourself you will inevitably enjoy yourself in the middle of actions too. Naturally the quality of your actions goes up and the results take care of themselves. If they don't... you don't mind... because you are already ENJOYING!

It's not necessarily about enjoying what you do, it's about **in-joying** yourself in the midst of whatever it is that you are doing. There is a big difference.

When we are always joyful in our natural state, we actually don't mind what happens and - this means we don't pay it any thought. We are not result orientated in order to be joyful. If things go our way great. If not... then that's ok too... as you are as still joyful either way.   This is a truly magnificent life changing reality to discover. To not **mind** what happens and to be joyful regardless of what does or does not occur is a huge unimaginable freedom to experience. It is an enormous realization to have, the consequences of which are huge, because it means we are experiencing **self-sufficient happiness!** Which most beings unfortunately never get to taste.

Often, in our culture we use words complacently, forgetting the real meaning behind those words. For example phrases such as, *'Mind where you are going,'* or *'Please mind your own business.'* We use the word *'mind'* a lot, yet tend to forget what it truly means not to **mind**.

When we say, *'Mind where you are going'*, it means *'think'* about where you are going. So to *'mind'* something means to *'think'* about something.

Often, people *'mind'* so many things...that when a person says something about them...they **mind** what is said. In other words, they ruminate, think and have an inner mental conversation and reaction about what has been said. Or another way of saying it is, they let the outside dictate how they feel and determine how they see themselves.

When a bill or payment demand is expected, they **mind** it. They think, worry, judge or have certain mental ideas about it. Instead, do not **mind** it so much. In other words, ignore what the mind says, as the mind only repeats the mental conditioning it holds – conditioning which is not you. Pay the mind little attention and stop taking thoughts so seriously.

To not **mind** something does not mean that you do not do anything about it, it simply means that you do not *'over-think'* it and thereby create a problem. Often the conditioned mind will find or create a problem. That is just the way it works, because one of its primary functions is problem solving, but many times there is no problem to be solved. If anything, it is the *'minding'* of something that creates a problem where none exists. In truth, there are no real problems in life, there are only situations to be handled. It is the mind which makes something a problem, and never the situation itself. Nature never sees a problem... only humans gripped by the programmed mind do.

If you truly wish to be tranquil, then stop *'minding'* what happens. So, when your romantic date does not arrive... do not **mind** this. Do not turn it into a problem by thinking about it or by regarding it as some reflection of who you are. It is not. It is not personal to you, because you are beyond the person, you are the **witnessing self**.

What a release and relief it is to be free from minding-... and free from the mind. With all the experiences and situations you face in your life, do not *'mind'* what happens. Stop *'over-thinking'* it and making it into an issue. Instead, be neutral towards it by looking from the witness who only sees **what is** as opposed to the mind which tries to interpret what is. Let your actions arise from this peaceful neutrality instead of the reactivity of the conditioned-self which is always looking to make things personal – and therefore a problem.

Just be aware of this and do not fall into its trap. Be neutral and do not *'mind'* what happens. What a beautiful freedom this is, to go through life unaffected and able to enjoy the world immensely without *'minding'*. What strength, being outside of the minds problem-creating nature, it imbues.

Practical Exercise: *So the practice is simple... do not mind what happens.*

If you do this one thing, then freedom will be yours eternally...

Another tendency the conditioned-self has in relation to taking action, is to be totally goal focused on a result rather than being presently aware of the moment and the task at hand within it.

When we are future oriented we are not fully present. When we are not fully present we often don't enjoy and engage fully with the action that we are doing because we are so eager to get to some future moment or result. This is what is known as **stress - *to restlessly pursue a result in the future to the detriment of your inner peace in the present.***

We can't be thinking of the future while we are taking action with the task at hand in the present. This only dilutes the quality of our actions and makes us feel restless in the process. Therefore, this thinking makes us want to get the action over and done with quickly so that we can skip straight to the result. A result that is not promised. A result we actually don't know will happen the way that we expect it to.

So the key to conscious action is to pay attention to the action knowing that your attentiveness will increase the quality of each action taken so that it creates a beautiful result in the next moment.

In other words, when we become intensely **present-based**, we feel centered at the core of our **being**, and from this beingness we begin to enjoy the process of acting in whatever form it takes. This significantly improves the quality of the action we take and therefore the result too. We both enjoy ourselves as well as performing to the best of our ability. It's a win win situation where nothing is sacrificed. So let go of thinking about the result and **fall in love** with the **process** instead. This is the *'joy of being'* in action.

Practical Exercise: *Notice how the mind clings to a future result in order to be happy. Instead, let go of the result and practice paying full attention to the action you are undertaking in the present.*

Fall in love with the **satisfied feeling** of being totally present in action. **In-joy** the state of being conscious in the midst of the action you partake in, and the results will take care of themselves. You will enjoy the ride along the way. Ultimately, what one will come to see is that you won't mind what happens... because you are so joyful. If things go your way... great, if not... then that's ok too. Either way you are still joyful.

In this state of being... no person or circumstance can take that away from you. From this realization, you will make all achieved results of secondary importance and your inner most joyful nature in the present primary. The trailer will no longer be placed before the truck.

21 – Alertness

When one has awoke to awakened-awareness, alertness serves to amplify your experience even more greatly. It opens the doors of perception a step further, and grounds you in that direct experience of pure presence.

Stay **highly alert** and you will directly experience a greater sense of wakefulness and vibrancy in each and every moment. Alertness pulls in more **aware presence** into your whole body.

Alertness is a heightened state of awareness and wakefulness which infuses us with an intense state of beingness. This alertness adds a kind of intensity to your experience of the body and the objects around you. It's like the doors of perception are flung wide open for you to intimately experience the present. Another way of describing alertness is - to be **intensely aware**. This alertness is a mental faculty that can be switched on and off at any moment, and it can aid in not falling back into unconsciousness and becoming lost in mind activity of the yesterday and tomorrow variety.

Aware-aliveness is life itself, whereas alertness is an added function of the brain. It is like having a normal light from a torch and then placing an extra device on it that amplifies it to an even brighter level. Alertness switches on the sensory organs to a greater level, and suddenly everything seems to become even more vibrant and alive. The faculties of the brain increase and your perception is greatly enhanced.

Practical Exercise: *If you ever feel yourself slipping back into the unconsciousness of mental noise and feel you are not present, then practice alertness. Don't focus on anything in particular, instead just widen your eyes slightly and be intensely awake and alert. Be in an intense state of hereness, which means the **sense of existing**, and stay relaxed as you do so.*

Wherever you are right now, scan around, without necessarily focusing on anything, but being more watchful in this moment. Very slightly widen the eyes.

As you do this you will find that the direct experience of being present and aware, magnifies greatly.

You may find all of your senses begin to heighten so that a deep richness of experience occurs. When you start to notice the mind becoming heavy and busy, just simply become more alert and wakeful of the immediate moment in front of you.

22 - Intensity of Action

One of the secrets of the enlightened beings is - they engage so totally in the action they are doing that they become it.

The key to creating powerful actions is to have full and total involvement in the action itself, so that the subject and object merge to become one cohesive force. When one is lost in the unconsciousness of thought, they have no real way to close the gap between the inner and outer. The medium of thought keeps them away from what they are engaging in, it keeps the subject away from the object.

All liberated beings have united with the one existence, or more accurately, they wake up from the dream of being a finite-identity that is separate from life, into a conscious realization of their totality once again. They move from a state of apartness to fullness. When this happens, anything they focus upon becomes absorbed by them, in them and as them. Subject and object becomes no more, and from this space a real power of action can happen. Suddenly it's as if life is occurring through you, rather than because of you.

The way to create intensity in action is to allow your attention to fixate fully on the task at hand and nothing but the task. To become so involved in what you are doing that you lose thoughts of anything else in the process. It is like an extreme sports athlete often engaging in these extreme sports because in that moment of heightened sensitivity and alertness they find **themselves** and they leave behind the burdening of the conditioned-self. They enter a temporary freedom from the mind.

In that moment of intense action, they lose the busyness of the mind and false self. It becomes highly addictive to them - to have a loss of the finite and be reintroduced with the aliveness of Infinite beingness. In this sense, they experience a momentary *'self-transcendence'*, where they feel free and boundless. However, this state never lasts for them, and so they go pursuing the activity again in the hope of feeling this newfound freedom. So similarly, one way that we can transcend the finite-self is through action. We do so by becoming totally involved and absorbed in what we are doing so much, that all sense of being a separate self fades far far into the background.

*Practical Exercise: Whatever you are doing, even if **doing** means you are doing nothing, become so involved in it that you lose the mind in the process.*

Pay **intense** attention to whatever you are doing so that you seem to merge and become one with it, where nothing else matters. Let the mind go. Keep the body relaxed as you do this.

By paying attention and staying fully involved in what you are doing, you inevitably cannot lose yourself in the unconsciousness of mind and therefore you will find yourself with a great sense of aliveness and watchfulness in what you do. This will make each action you take a conscious and joyful one. When the *'medium'* of the mind between **who you are** and **what you do** collapses, you will become one with reality and align with its Infinite flow. This is a true spiritual union.

The universe bends to the one who is both surrender-red and who is intensely involved with what they are doing. Give every action your fullest attention and beautiful achievements and feats will occur, as well as explosions of joy. It's magick.

23 - Life is Not a Game

Life is not a game but instead a mystery and play to be enjoyed and lived. Games are always reserved for the bored and life is only for those that are awake.

Life is a play not a game. A game is always a win and lose scenario and always based in the duality of the mind. That is, my winning depends on you losing, and your winning depends on me losing. There is no real winner or loser in life, because you are **life!** What could you possibly win and what could you possibly lose?!

All are just ideas spiraling around in the mind and not in the fabric of existence. But if we believe winning and losing to be real, then for us it becomes so. All is but a play in the same way that actors play on the stage. They play the character and realize that they are ultimately not the character at the same time.

They play the character to the fullest and may even at times lose themselves in the role, but at the core they know they are not essentially that which they play. This existence is like a dance of various forces. When one dances at a disco, they do not dance to compete with another dancer, they dance because they enjoy dancing and they want to flow with the rhythm. Enjoy life and dance your dance, sing your song and don't be concerned with comparing your song to another's.

Come to see life as a play and not a game. When you **play** you experience the **joy of being** in the **present**. However, when you think it is a game you are always in the future trying to be somewhere else other than here. Play… and the world will play with you. Compete… and life will always push against you.

The conditioned-self is always looking to acquire more because it believes it is in a reality of lack. It believes it is separate from the rest of life and that it has to gather as much stuff for itself, even if that means others have to lose so that it can win. The finite-self believes it is always in a game with life - and so it is always strategizing the future to try and be successful. Instead, simply relax the strategies and live spontane-ously. To live spontaneously means to allow for what arises in your **being** in this moment to spring forth and be expressed. Who are you in this moment?

What freshly bubbles to the surface from your inner silence in this moment?

When you let go and just be... what comes forth in each moment?

It is a mystery, and to allow that mystery to be lived is true spontaneity.

Plan, but always be spontaneous and flexible in your plan. Play, sing, dance and celebrate life, and watch how this will be infectious to others. Remember, there is nothing to be won or gained, nor is there anything to truly lose. Just play the play and enjoy the ride along the way.

24 - Reverence

Having a deep appreciation for existence is the purest kind of prayer.

The act of reverence and appreciation is a conscious action that brings us into harmony with life *'as it is'* through an embrace and acknowledgment of its nature. When we have a deep love for life, which means we have come to see existence's benevolent friendly nature, then we cannot help but become more conscious in the moment and in our actions, because we are not looking towards the future for more... or back in the past for what we feel we didn't get. Instead we are truly seeing and loving what is here in the present. We are loving **what is**, then life takes on a whole new experience for us. Maybe for the very first time... we are loving what is **now** and who we truly are in this moment. Life is kind, because even the harshest appearing challenges are a gift from existence for us. They are there to dispel the ultimate illusion *(separation)* and come back into alignment with the truth of our self which is one with the Universe as the Supreme Being.

Unfortunately, without these challenges, many beings would remain in ignorance of their real nature and only suffer for longer periods and maybe even indefinitely, because if nothing arises to wake you up from your slumber... then you may remain sleeping for eternity!

Out of compassion, the universe gives us whatever we need to *'wake up'*, and when we no longer need it... then it no longer needs to give us those challenges. When energy is out of alignment in a system, just the same way a body may be in dis-ease, then a symptom will come along to grab our attention. Our body is saying **'look, pay attention! You are out of alignment, and this is going to cost you now and further down the line!'** In other words, the Universe, just like the body, is trying to assist you in coming back into harmony with yourself *(the Infinite)*.

Out of shear intelligence, it gives you a sign in the form of a symptom so that you can hear the message and correct the misalignment. In the very same way, as the Universe is a macrocosm of the body, it too is seeking to gain your attention so that you can correct your disharmony and move back in alignment with it. So how do you move back into alignment with life?

You dispel the illusions that are appearing to keep you out of its flow. In other words, it is a call back to reality, a call back to the truth of yourself which is one with the Infinite universe. Every time something challenging happens, it is a **wakeup call!** You are being asked to pay attention and find out what attachments, illusions or sense of separateness you are holding on to. Challenges are a time to stop and reflect, to find what is real and true.

When you deeply contemplate and see that the universe is always spurring you on to truth, in ways that may often seem too mysterious and harsh to the conditioned mind, but that nevertheless brings opportunity to correct, then a gratitude for life will be with you in every moment. The sacredness of existence will open to you and your life will be filled with prayer. Not a prayer of which you beg and wish for more (*this is not true prayer as life has already given you enough*), but true prayer being the quality of life's grace and kindness realized in you. It is seeing the already full nature of life, its kind nature, and what life brings you to awaken to the truth beyond the fickle nature of the phenomenal world.

Thankfulness is the highest prayer, because it is a way to show love to the eternal: the eternal being your undiluted self, pure and clean. Your own being is looking after you... itself, always doing what is necessary for you to awaken. It is like the Zen Master who may whack his students with a stick in order for them to become instantly aware and awaken. It may look harsh from the outside but the cost of momentary suffering is a small price to pay for everlasting truth and freedom. The Universe knows all and sees all, because it is all, including you. The universe will not let you rest until you come back home to your inherent freedom. When we understand this, we will be thankful for all opportunities life brings us. Even if we cannot be immediately grateful, eventually we will look back and say – thank you!

Practical Exercise: *Say 'thank you' often. Take a moment and find things in the immediate present to be appreciative for. Health, food, nature and so on. Embrace your surroundings and all within it.*

If you can't find anything to be grateful for because you feel resistance coming from the mind, then just get on your knees, put your hands together and say thank you. Keep saying it.

In this prayer position you cannot be arrogant, and something will open. Watch the energy lift within you.

For instance, even if you are homeless and have no material possessions, you can still be grateful for the clothes on your back, for stars above your head and the floor beneath your feet.

You can still be appreciative of a simple act of kindness from a stranger or a small drink or piece of food you have. Life provides us plenty, it is all around us. All we have to do is tune into it and give it our thanks and respect. Just keep saying **'thank you'**, because when you do you will find yourself noticing more things to be thankful for.

The energy of thankfulness and reverence brings a greater sense of hereness and cleans you from the inside out, because essentially thanking the whole of existence is also paying homage to our own true self. Being thankful is a quality of the heart, and when our heart opens to existence, that is what gets reflected to us. If we show our heart, then existence shows the heart of itself to us, and in that moment we consciously become one with it.

The more wisdom we gain from our experiences of trusting the universe and seeing how what it brings is a way to transform us, the more grateful we will feel and the more we will enjoy the growth and expansion of our enlightenment and freedom.

Life is like a mirror. When you open your arms and embrace it, life will give you a big hug.

Section 5
Devotion & Surrender To The Infinite - The Final Enlightened Liberation

25 - The Meaning of Devotion & Surrender

Fall in love with the Infinite and let go of the finite.

Devotion and surrender both together or individually can lead to final **Enlightened Liberation**. Final Enlightened Liberation means that you no longer live in unconsciousness or ignorance. No longer do you suffer or are bound by self-imposed limitations, you have transcended the finite-self and have fully awoken to the Infinite-Self. There is no going back from final Enlightened Liberation. Once subject and object become one and union has occurred, you are forever free and forever one with the eternal Infinite-Self.

Devotion is the way of committing one's life to the highest, that being the Infinite source of existence, which is presently here now residing in you. The word *'God'* was often used in ancient traditions, however because of its conceptual baggage I will instead call it the *'Eternal'* or the *'Infinite'*. When we turn our attention away from the conditioned-self and place it towards the eternal, we are practicing the art of devotion.

Devotion means we must fall in love with our meditation practice. We must fall in love with existence, our eternal source nature, and we must seek to rest and be one with the Isness... the Infinite.

The Infinite eternal essence of existence is the true self at the core of your being: and so every time you are in your meditation, which simply means to be presently aware and not unconsciously lost in thought, you are committing yourself to the highest. Each time you are consciously aware in the present, you are opening yourself up to a beautiful blossoming of your true nature and in this you are devoting yourself to reality. When one is being a conditioned-identity, you are out of sync with the universe, but as soon as you touch the Infinite within, you are instantaneously aligned with the totality of life once again. Spiritual process means: *coming back into harmony with the Isness of life.*

Surrender means that we are continuously dropping identification with the conditioned mind and are instead, staying consciously rooted in the Infinite-Self. Surrender means we are trusting the Infinite and not the programmed mind. To go to the experience of the Infinite-Self, we simply look from the position of the **witnessing presence** behind our eyes... You cannot see the self, but you can see that you are already seeing from that place...

The conditioned-self is always seeking to control life on an independent basis. It sees and experiences itself as a separate entity from life. Surrender means we are ending the struggle the mind creates in reaction and resistance to what life brings, and instead we are letting go of control and allowing life to operate through us. We surrender ourselves to the will of the

Infinite universe and in the process become one with its natural movement - just the same way that a seemingly independent wave sees that it is not apart from the ocean it sits in and came from, and therefore effortlessly rests back into its flow. Surrender means a willingness to allow life to happen as it is... without pushing up against it. It takes a lot of effort to push... but no effort at all to let go. In surrender, we meet everything just as it is, and we trust what life brings.

In other words, we surrender the will of the conditioned-self in replace of the will of the universe (*Infinite-Self*). It's like an armistice: we hand over everything that is not truly us. We surrender and relinquish all of ourselves over into the arms of the one beloved eternal existence. That is true surrender, a true letting go. All illusions get handed over in replace of only that which is real and pure.

26 - Freedom From Experience vs Freedom In Experience

Ultimate freedom does not come in the absence of existence, but by you being the absence that holds all existence within it.

There will come a time when... no matter what you practice... or however watchful, aware or present you are, that no amount of that will stop you from experiencing the inevitable. Sometimes something may be so deeply rooted in identification that suffering will undoubtedly come, and in these moments, we must face and transcend the experience by going **into it** rather than trying to be the witness of it.

Some experiences (*thoughts, feelings and circumstances*) will arise that are much easier to view from a distance with a sense of spaciousness, while other experiences may feel as though they are right on top of you pressing up against your face. These are the experiences that we must meet directly and go into, in order to defeat them. They are screaming for our attention, they are shouting to be acknowledged and healed through the love and embrace of our heartfelt presence. We can transform them by welcoming their presence, as opposed to trying to keep them away. This is true alchemy. Our alchemy is to dissolve these experiences by touching and meeting them with the loving embrace of our heartfelt presence. This automatic inclusion of all experiences is the basis and result of our union with the totality of existence: the true oneness and nondual nature of life.

Practical Exercise: *Whatever you feel in this moment, whether that be fear, guilt, shame, grief, stress, worry or negativity, do you have the willingness to allow it in and for you to be with it in this moment? Can you open to what comes as opposed to closing? Can you let go of resistance and instead be with whatever you feel in this moment?*

We find freedom in experience by inviting the experience in, and through the willingness to meet what arises with allowance and presence in this moment. Often people are resisting certain feelings and emotions, usually because they perceive these things as being bad or negative. However this discrimination of what is a 'good' or 'bad' is purely social conditioning we have been taught. In the Western world especially, we are often taught to move away from anything unpleasant at all costs. It is the struggle of running away from these things that is the real culprit of our prolonged suffering, for if we were willing to face what comes in this moment, we would discover the capacity within to be able to hold and take everything that comes across our path. Not only would we discover our ability to hold and take them, but that in the absence of struggling against them, they dissolve in the energy of our presence. The more we resist, the more we become closed, and by closing we suffer.

What if instead you stayed open and allowed whatever comes to come, and whatever goes to go?

All of our suffering, unhappiness and misery comes when we close to what enters our present moment experience. As soon as resistance hits...turmoil occurs instantly. We find freedom not in running away, but in meeting the experience at hand, and the way to meet it is through non-judgmental allowance of it. If sadness comes let it come. It will go of its own accord provided we are not feeding it with judgement and resistance. All experiences including thoughts and feelings are fickle. They are always arriving and leaving without our invitation or dismissal of them. We have no control what we think or feel, but we do control how open, present and aware we are in response to the different thoughts and feelings that will inevitably come. The more we stay as that open awareness, which means to have conscious awareness of the present, the more thoughts and feelings get dissolved in it. In this way we discover deep freedom in everything that life can bring our way. What could be more beautiful and powerful than that?

This is your natural freedom, this is your original nature.

27 - Transcending Fear

Fear is always a projection of mind into the morrow.

The finite-self loves to know what is in the following moment because it seeks full control. It seeks control because it fears being out of control and being out of control could mean its annihilation. Mental fear happens when we think and imagine the future. Fear can never happen in the present because as soon as we are lost in thinking we seem to lose the experience of the present. Whilst lost in thought...we are not consciously experiencing that which is presently here.

Practical Exercise: *Stay in the direct experience of **now**. Fear cannot happen in this moment it can only happen by thinking of the next moment.*

Fear is always about something of which is not in our immediate experience of now. Fear can only come by thinking of what the future may be. It's an assumption...that's all. Don't indulge in thinking about the unknown of which is not in this moment, instead just be here now. Be the **witness** to fear...not the owner of it. Stay with your direct experience of **now** and not with a mental image or script of tomorrow. Direct experience is the real and the imagined is always the unreal. The former is what is actually occurring in reality and the latter is just a mental projection happening in the head. When we confuse the image and our thoughts for truth, we suffer. The way out of unhappiness is to discover: what is a fact and what is a fiction.

Notice that you are not the fearful thought itself, you are the one who can witness it. Witness the fear and notice how it fades when you do not feed it with the energy of identification and belief. In other words, just witness the fear and don't identify with it. Don't see it as who you are, as it is not who you are. You are deeper than that, and you are the witnessing of it in which it happens. The feeling of fear is just at the surface. It is happening whilst you are looking at it from underneath and beyond...

Often times through the mind we imagine and assume something will definitely happen, but ultimately we cannot know one hundred percent. Nothing is certain. Most of the time what we specifically think, and what actually happens are two different things. So for this reason, it is better to stay present and not try to anticipate the next instance.

Because if we do... we imagine all kinds of scenarios that may never happen, and then all we will have done is create stressful feelings for no reason. How many times have you thought something was going to turn out a specific way... only to find that it turned out completely differently?

If you are honest with yourself, you will see this has happened many many times. As you can therefore see, nobody can ultimately know the future. It's unpredictable and based on so many different factors, people and circumstances that are outside of our control. And even if one could know the future, why worry about that which is not here?

When it comes... it will come as the present, allowing us to deal and accept it presently. So stop assuming or expecting of 'what is to come'. Start living in the direct experience of now.

When a fearful thought is believed it creates a response in the body that we call an 'emotion' or 'feeling'. It is often this feeling that tends to overwhelm a person, as the feelings can often feel more sticky or heavy than the thoughts. A thought can arise, but if it is not believed then there is no problem, it will just pass. However, a thought believed creates a bodily reaction within you, and this reaction becomes a feeling or emotion. Luckily, you are not the body: you are deeper than that. You are prior to the body's formation. So when the feeling is noticed, we simply relax into the sensation as opposed to struggling against it. We open and allow its presence to be there rather than closing and resisting it.

Instead of trying to move a million miles away from these feelings, we allow ourselves to bring our conscious awareness into the heart of it. Not a millimeter either side of it... but right in the centre. In this way we shine a loving healing light upon it - just as the sun shines its warm caressing light upon our face.

Practical Exercise: *Stay with the feeling that the fearful thought produces. Instead of struggling or identifying with it...**surrender** to it, which means, quit fighting it. Instead, experience it fully without judgement.*

The tendency we have, is to fear the fearful feeling itself, which is the real cause of our suffering. Instead of seeking to avoid it, give yourself permission to go into the feeling, to embrace it and experience it fully. Do not mentally judge it or create a story about it. Do not make it right or wrong... good or bad, instead just feel it by placing your **silent watchfulness** upon it. See what happens...

Stay present with it and watch it fade...

The conditioned-self has been programmed to move away from anything unpleasant at all costs, and so it seems illogical to come into the feeling that appears to be giving us unpleasantness. In actuality however, it has the opposite effect to what the conditioned-self thinks...

The suffering that we experience does not come from the feeling itself, it comes from our **struggle** against the feeling. Resisting the feeling and wanting it to stop or go away is the very thing that makes us suffer. So when we **accept** and **relax into** the feeling with a total watchfulness of it... it transforms. By not struggling against the feeling we are experiencing in the moment... we automatically end suffering because we drop the *'middle man'* *(conditioned self/mind)* and find the freedom we are after in the midst of it.

Whatever fear arises, do not resist it. Instead accept it and experience it totally, and you will be free. This is how all fears are transcended. This is how all suffering is transmuted into a greater **aware presence**.

28 - Nonidentity

Stop attaching and identifying yourself as the temporary and limited.

Ones bondage as the **finite-identity** is born because the infinite *(who we really are)* has been taught to always associate who it is with the things of the temporary and limited world.

Identifying as the temporary and limited means that you go from the direct experience of being Infinite and feeling boundless... to a finite object that is limited in time and space, and at the core of this finite-self is a sense of separation that becomes apparent within the experience of the one who is identified with it. The moment you say that *'I am this'* or *'I am that'*, you put a cap and limitation on the Infinite core of that which is looking out from beneath your eyes, and that which is looking is **free objectless intelligence** *(the Infinite-Self)*. Who you are is **objectless** because it cannot be encapsulated in a concept or referred to as a physical form: it is beyond all conditions and limits. It has no border, boundary or edge that can define it.

The very second you try to define yourself, you put up imaginary metal bars that keep you bound and subject to that definition, and in doing so, you lose the direct experience and feeling of the Infinite-Self. So the practice is very simple: stop identifying and defining who you are with finite objects. This also includes ceasing to identify with experiences both internally and externally, because the world of experiences is the world of objects and form.

Practical Exercise: *Watch how the mind is always associating with certain objects for its sense of self. Refrain from these limitations by not becoming identified with anything in particular.*

Stay as the space which holds everything but is not limited to something specific.

Question what is finite and what is Infinite, and when you have seen all that is finite in both the so called 'internal' and 'external world' then cease to identify with it. Don't acquire your sense of self from it.

What will be left can only be the **Infinite-Self** that you truly are. The Infinite-Self cannot be seen, because it is not an object, but you can recognize that you are watching from that place and then begin to watch the watching watch...

As long as the conditioned-self has a mental concept to rest on and identify with, you will never truly be free. All mind associations must go in order for true unlimited freedom to be directly experienced.

29 - Absolute Cooperation with Isness

True freedom is when you quit struggling and allow everything to be just as it is.

If there is only one practice or teaching that would suffice for Enlightenment and Liberation it would be this - **to have absolute cooperation with the Isness of life.** Which is to say, just be available to whatever is happening without any inner resistance. Let it move in…and let it move out freely, without trying to stop or hold what life brings, and without judging what shows up within that experience *(i.e. events, thoughts and feelings).*

Absolute cooperation with **Isness** is a state of being that is in total alignment with life **as it is** in this moment. Everything that has happened to this point is what the universe has brought. It can be no other way than what it is right now. However, many people through their identification with mind and their expectations, hopes and dreams want things to be different than how life is right now in this moment. Because of this want for things to be different, people tend to struggle and consequently cause suffering for themselves.

To go beyond this self-induced suffering caused by the inner struggle against this present moment, we must come into a state of **total allowance** and be in harmony with life **as it is** in the now. When we allow the moment to be as it is, as if we have given it permission to be this way, then our whole being will sync with existence and we experience a state of inner harmony. When we struggle however - buying into a mental story of resistance to the situation in our head – then we suffer: falling back into a state of unawareness *(belief in thought).*

So if we accept this moment with every fiber of our being, without any thought-based opposition, then a deep peace will fall upon us. In this way, we are in complete cooperation with life, and then existence becomes our best friend and greatest ally. Tranquility spontaneously creeps upon us.

Practical Exercise: *Quit struggling with **what is** and align your whole being with the oneness of the life by having total acceptance and allowance of how everything is in this moment. One hundred percent acceptance of the present.*

In other words, when we stop struggling against how things are in this moment, we find an immediate sense of ease that occurs. It is like ice melting back into the ocean. No longer are we suffering... because no longer are we struggling. No inner struggle means no suffering. No suffering means peace... peace turns into joy and joy turns into love... and love can turn into bliss and even ecstasy!

To resist how things are in this moment makes no sense, because it is already the case: it has already happened. The only thing that makes sense, is for us to come into harmony with how things are right now through acceptance and allowance. When we cease struggling we will feel a sudden tranquility and relaxation that occurs, and suddenly we gain an unbelievable sense of freedom that is incomeprehensible to the intellect.

The whole universe has brought the substance of this moment to how it is right now. To resist would mean we are pushing against the entire movement of existence. It is too much pressure for the mind to bear. However, if we **let go**, we would immediately find ourselves in total alignment with life and its supreme power and intelligence.

Let go of resistance and accept this moment wholeheartedly and completely with every fiber of your being and you will directly experience unimaginable liberation in all facets of your life. **Or more accurately you will experience life as life itself**. And as life is everything and no-thing you are no longer bound by any one thing. You will bloom like a beautiful flower and radiate a scent of pure joy moment to moment. When the **beingness** is not obstructed by the coiled-up inner resistance of thoughts believed, its natural brightness always shines through effortlessly and immediately.

30 - Experience of the Infinite Drop

Freedom is found in the midst of each experience by dropping deeply into it. This is spiritual alchemy.

We find true freedom not by trying to get away from life but by dropping our whole being evermore deeply into it. Often times the finite-self is seeking something other than what is here, and it wishes to be elsewhere experiencing something different. It wants to avoid certain situations, thoughts and feelings at all costs which becomes the bane of its suffering and dis-harmony with life.

Stop avoiding what shows up and show up with it fully. Learn to sit with whatever comes. Be with any situation and experience by letting go of avoidance and dropping deeper into everything life brings. When you try to avoid or move away from life you split yourself in two. However, when you show up fully, you become **one** with whatever is occurring in the present. In doing so you transmute each experience into yourself *(the Supreme-Being)* and you breathe the life of the Infinite into it. In this way each experience is transformed into the **pure conscious presence** of who you really are. This is true conscious alchemy at the highest level.

Practical Exercise: *Allow yourself to drop deeply into every experience without exception. Face it head on and go into it with a full presence of openness.*

Keep it as it is...don't seek to change it. Fall evermore deeply into each present experience that arises. It is as if you are falling through yourself into yourself. It is like space floating through space. It is a total free-fall in which you are the body and the sky in which the body is falling simultaneously.

Total absorption in every experience without exception is pure freedom and empowerment. It is a true communion with the physical and nonphysical dimensions of one's experience.

The deeper you drop into your present experience, the more the physical and nonphysical merge and expand in tandem. This creates an opening into a dimension of stillness and groundedness at the centre of existence: this centre being at the core of you. This conscious openness infuses everything with a sweet flavor of existential intimacy beyond intellectual capacity.

Let go and drop further and further into every present experience that arises...

31 - Trusting Infinite Intelligence

The conditioned-self says 'show me and I'll trust you' the infinite-self says 'trust me and I'll show you'.

One of the biggest barriers to trust is fear. Fear that comes from a sense of personhood in the conditioned state. However, when one steps out of the person into the vastness of the true self, trust becomes natural and effortless, because it is recognized that trusting life is the same as trusting yourself. Life is the bigger **YOU**, so why would life not wish to align with itself?

Why would it not wish for itself to succeed in expansion and growth? A growth that is only possible when it supports you in the direct realization of your original self?

As we move along the spiritual path towards Self-Realization and Liberation, or from the head into the heart, many fears and doubts may arise. These fears are normal and are generated by the programmed mind in an attempt to keep its finite-identity intact and regain a sense of *'personal'* control. Just the same way as a nervous passenger will try to take hold of the steering wheel of a moving car... for fear of death.

As life moves along and unfolds, the conditioned-self will also become scared and wish to interject for fear of what may or may not happen.

In fact, the conditioned-self is always deeply scared at its core and that is because it's in a fight for survival all of the time. It has a sense of being separate from life and so it seeks to control all that it can, so as to not be harmed or completely destroyed by things it perceives as separate from itself.

In this perception, everything can seem like a threat to

its existence - which means it is always living in some kind of perpetual fear beneath the surface. This is why it is constantly throwing up stressful thoughts - all in an attempt to protect itself.

This is fine, so long as we recognize that it is the last 'gasps of breath' of the finite-identity. For when we do, we can surrender the identity of those thoughts and allow them to dissolve in their own time, and leave them to preach to themselves.

When one sets out on the journey of Self-Realization- ...all the forces in the universe come to assist you in that discovery.

To awaken to the truth of who you really are as the Secret-Self is a most auspicious affair, as it leads to many secrets of the universe being revealed to you. All secrets coming to you in the presence of yourself in the immediate moment of now. The secrets are seen- ...not learnt. They are directly experienced and not intellectually accumulated.

The truth is not something that is given, because that means it could also be taken away. Instead the truth is revealed as the universe supports you in peeling away the layers of illusion you were once blinded by before. As the truth unfolds within you, life is there, backing and supporting your every realization.

Allow yourself to surrender and trust the unfolding that is taking place both externally and internally in your life. It is all unfolding as it should. Life is helping to untie the knots that have formed within you - all you have to do is get out of the way through your daily practice... and existence will take care of the rest.

The Supreme-Being is the vast intelligent space that holds the whole of existence together. It can see the bigger picture whereas the mind can only see pieces. You are this intelligent space. You are the vast Infinite-Self. To trust it is to also trust yourself, and if you do, it will prove itself to you time and time again. Trust is easy, and often we are always trusting something. We trust that our plane ride will get to its destination safely and on time, we trust that the food we eat hasn't been tampered with, and we trust that we won't lose our job so that we can continue to pay for our weekly expenses. Almost all encounters of our daily lives are based on trust, so why not trust the very thing that supports all of the other things we trust? Why not trust the source of intelligence that everything sprang out of... and everything is being held together by?

Instead of trusting the programmed mind, put your faith in the **all-knowing supreme intelligence** of existence - that which gave birth to everything. It knows what is in your heart of hearts and is always seeking to guide you back to the heart so that you can live from that space and see the truth of existence. It knows you more intimately than you know yourself whilst in the conditioned state. The universe will never stop supporting you and is always guiding you back home to the Infinite. If you trust it, then you allow its grace to enter your life consciously. If you trust the mind however, you will be deceived over and over again - which will only induce more suffering and ignorance within your life.

That which is finite is the illusion and Infinity is the truth. Surrender to the Infinite and trust the truth of who you really are in this moment: that being the immortal essence which is all that is and dwells in all things.

You are the Infinite born out of itself... experiencing itself.

32 - Unequivocal Surrender to the Infinite

Surrender is when the wave realizes it is the ocean and rests in its flow.

A wave on its own is not as powerful as the ocean that gave birth to it. If the wave came into conscious unison with the ocean it would flow with ease and gain its true power, intelligence and momentum. The same is so for the Infinite as it recognizes itself through us and surrenders to its inherent universal home.

Surrender simply means - **to surrender the illusion of that which is not you: the conditioned-self.** For the finite-self, the word *'surrender'* can appear scary. The word can often be seen as a way of giving-up or quitting something - something that the Western culture tends to pride itself in *'not doing'*. But essentially, surrender has nothing to do with giving-up something externally, or giving up a certain action. Rather it has everything to do with handing-over that which is not you: the illusion. This illusion which is not you, are the ideas you have about who you are and how things should be. Essentially, what you are not: is the mind. You are not the idea you have of yourself, you stretch far beyond that.

If there is a giving-up of anything, it is a giving-up of the illusion that we are a separate finite-self, a mind/body identity made up of thoughts. The mind that believes it is a separate self will often jockey for control in many of life's situations. This creates struggle, and as a result we often suffer unnecessarily, all because the finite-self feels it needs to control life through the fear-based projections it carries.

There will come a time when all practices and strategies fail and only the occurrence of **unequivocal surrender** will suffice. The application of practice is always first initiated by the intermediary of mind, because you must use the mind to re-mind yourself to practice. However, there will come a time when we move deeply into a 'complete' Enlightenment *(full-consciousness)* without any aid from thought. This has to happen otherwise there will always be some Illusionary identity left that is trying to steer and control things, which will inevitably keep one in the realm of the finite-self. Therefore, eventually the role of the *'practicer'* or *'meditator'* will have to leave, for how can you practice being yourself?

How can you practice being your true nature of which is Infinite and free?

You can't practice being yourself...otherwise you will definitely NOT be yourself. It's like asking someone to act natural. If someone tries to act natural they will become more and more unnatural each time they try. So you cannot practice being yourself. **You are yourself already**. Just simply be you, or more accurately, stop trying or using effort to be anything other than what is inherently natural at your core. Be no more expressive than your true nature.

You can only practice being more conscious, however the final straw of being totally conscious means to entirely drop all unconsciousness, which includes the finite mind that *'thinks'* it needs to be more conscious and practice. Practice needs time to get there, while in actuality only the absence of time will suffice. This means we must drop the approach to become enlightened in the future and instead surrender to the infinite in the present, as enlightenment is always now.

In other words, the 'thought' that one needs to be more conscious is actually the finite mind speaking and that very thought is a blockage. Underneath that, you have always been conscious. You have always been Infinite under the illusionary disguise of being finite. This means that eventually the demand to practice will... in and of itself... be the last barrier to 'Total Enlightenment'. All practices and strategies of the mind will have to be put away and what will remain is that which can't be practiced or refined: pure objectless intelligence *(the Infinite-Self)*.

The floodgates to Infinite only open when the control and will of the finite is let go of and is no more.

You see, our true nature is that of being **ONE** with the whole of existence. How can we be one and flow with all of existence if we insist that we are a separate entity with our own finite agenda?

How can we flow and merge in union with the totality of life if we are always trying to control life and people for individualist ego gain and *'personal'* benefit?

How can we be available to receive what the supreme intelligence wishes to give us through its grace and support, if we allow the finite conditioned self to dictate what is best for us?

How can we be set free into the Infinite if we are attached to the limited and finite?

What is being asked in surrender is the surrender of the *'person'* and not the true-self: the surrender of the illusion and not the reality. There are no levels of surrender - either we surrender or we do not. It is not something that is done, it is simply a truth to be realized and tasted in the present. It is the direct experience of coming into contact with reality in the present. Surrender is the realization that we are not the finite mind and its wants, needs and struggles, and when we recognize this we will drop the illusion.

When we are exhausted and tired of battling-with and engaging in the finite mind's antics, we will soon let it go and be done with it. If something is too heavy to carry... you drop it! You don't keep picking it back up and exhausting yourself, it makes no sense. The minds programming is too much for a being to bear for long. The list of its programs are growing by the day, all based on untruth. Eventually it must be dropped, so why not now?

The conditioned-self will hold on out of fear, never realizing that the holding on (*attachment*) is the very thing that is generating the fear in the first place. If one would only let go... fear would be over and freedom would reign supreme.

When our sufferings and self-limitations seem too

unbearable and illusions dominate us, use this as the moment to quit fighting and surrender. **Let go**.

The more and more we 'let go', the more and more we will effortlessly flow. To let go means to simply realize the truth, relax and surrender and just be the Infinite and boundless being that you are. Just be free. Allow yourself to merge and melt back into the existence that is all around you and within you. In surrender we must face death and be willing to die, and to die in each moment. It is the only sure way that we can truly live, because as long as we hold on to fear we cannot truly live. We will always be scared and shrink in the face of life.

Fear shrinks, but truth expands you: it is boundless.

We must be willing to let go of all that which we have believed to be true about ourselves and life up to this point, otherwise we cannot enter the gateless gate which leads into eternal life itself. You cannot live in truth if you already 'think' you know it. Your belief keeps you in the mind... but reality can only be entered through the absence of mind. How can we freefall into existence if we are desperately holding onto the handles of the door?

How can we feel the beauty of the ocean if we are only willing to dip our toe in and then shy away?

You must be willing to jump, to dive, to immerse yourself all the way. It is all or nothing. It's truth or illusion, freedom or suffering: your choice?

Do not try to surrender, pretend to surrender, or even surrender just a little. We either surrender or we do not. We either resist or we flow. We either struggle or we cease to struggle. We cannot be half within a sense of finite identity and half within the Infinite-Self at the same time. We are either in **complete let go**... or we are not. There is no in-between.

Either we realize the truth and are free, or we continue believing ourselves to be the illusion and continue to suffer. So, surrender to the reality of which you truly are and unite back into the eternal embrace of the single Infinite existence.

Move spontaneously in a state of total let go, allowing yourself to be animated only by the eternal, and that will only come when we are totally surrendered to the Infinite.

Stop believing the thoughts that run through your head... and internally do nothing...expect nothing and be free...

Relax and surrender into the arms of the beloved divine intelligence. Allow it to guide you, as it will.

Allow yourself to float in the waters of the universe

and your own being. The wave remembering and recognizing itself as the entire ocean...

33 - Your Job is Simple

*Your job is simple: just **be** and **allow** all else to be **as it is.***

Whether we wish to call it a purpose or just simply living our true nature, our **job** is actually very simple, because if it was complicated we would quickly become lost and fall back into the clutches of the mind-identity once again. Only the conditioned-self makes things more complicated than it needs to be, and it can easily turn everything into an intellectual problem solving process that takes time *(illusory time)* to accomplish. However the truth takes no time at all... it is just now! You are now!

Awakening is just the approach of recognizing you are aware and noticing this moment and who you are within it... that is it. Who are you in this moment? Consciously look from those eyes, the one who is aware right now within you...

The more aware you are... the more awake you are, and when all unawareness has been cast away, freedom will naturally be there.

There is nothing to do, instead only *be-ing* remains. To **be** may seem like a practice, but all that is happening is to not be unconscious. As far as our Self-Realization goes, and us being more solidified in that realization, all we must allow to happen is **present moment awareness** and **letting go** and **allowance** of whatever comes and whatever goes... as it is taking place within our direct experience in the present. It sounds like you must do something, but in reality it is the opposite. It is actually a *non-doing*. It is only the mind that does something. It is only the mind that moves, but you don't budge even an inch. How far away from yourself could you possibly be?

Not even an atom I assure you.

Many beings have been **doing** unawareness, *but* **conscious witnessing** *is always present, as without it you would* not be able to be aware of reading this book right now, or of sitting in a seat.

Our job is to simply **relax** and allow everything to occur by itself in the immediate moment, even to allow witnessing to occur by itself, as it is doing already, I challenge you to try and stop it....

Impossible!

I challenge you to not be in the present moment...

Impossible.

It is already happening by itself, and it cannot be stopped. Seeing this brings one consciously to the direct experience of the natural-self. In the place of the true natural-self, joy, clarity and all beautiful qualities arise, and it is from the true-self that the gift is given.

What gift is this, you ask?

Well, you. You are the gift. Not necessarily what is being done, but in all certainty what you ARE... is the gift. Wherever you are at *(in terms of awakening and your level of awareness)*, just be it and express it naturally as you feel. No more and no less: simply express no more than what is your true nature in each given moment. As you go deeper into the true reality of the present moment and that which is beyond thoughts, that expression will mature and change accordingly to synchronize with life in a harmonious way.

Surrender and cooperate with life **as it is**. Be consciously aware of the hereness of the moment. In other words, just simply **be** and **allow** all else to be...that is it. That is the whole teaching - a teaching that if realized will bring about a total Enlightenment and freedom beyond intellectual understanding. A freedom that is with you right here and now. By realizing this teaching or pointing, one will defeat the ancient battle within, simply by means of making peace with the mind. When you conquer the battle within...you will never have to face a battle outside of yourself ever again. Mastery of the self is mastery of the world: this is the secret of true world peace. True world peace will never start as an outer phenomenon, it will always begin within the hearts of each individual.

As surrender to deeper and deeper levels occurs, more and more of the Secret-Self will emerge and be expressed naturally. It cannot be contained! Be yourself and live purposefully in the reality of the here and now. Do whatever feels right in your heart and enjoy the unfolding mystery before you. Live in the recognition that there is only ever the present. Live fearlessly by knowing that the body could drop at any moment. Existence is uncertain, so live each moment as if it is your last, because one day it inevitably will be. To know that is truly liberating, as you will live more intensely and joyfully than most beings ever have before. In this realization life will be your eternal playground in which to be joyful and live from the heart.

In the direct knowing of your true nature, you will have a feeling of being one with all things. Of living in this realization and having the experience that humanity is an extension of you. Of being a walking gift to all with whom you come into contact. Be empty, it's the only sure way to be full: full of life, love, infinity and humanity in your heart. Give freely like the year-round fruit bearing tree, knowing you will never run out.

There is only one. You are that one Infinite-Being, which is the source of all things. Enjoy the ride.

About the Author

Christopher J. Smith is a Meditation Teacher and Mystic who is dedicated to serving humanity with self-transformational tools, and inner technologies, that are based in new science and ancient spiritual practice.

He lives in South Yorkshire England, and travels around the world where he shares spirituality, meditation, empowerment and human wellbeing practices.

To learn more about Christopher, or contact him, visit:

- Christopher J Smith on Youtube
- Silent Truth on Facebook
- lifesynergyhealth@gmail.com
- www.lifesynergyhealth.co.uk

27577984R00102

Printed in Great Britain
by Amazon